VIRGINIA
WOOLF

ART, LIFE AND VISION

For Judy, from one of your admiring students Gail Shane

VIRGINIA WOOLF

ART, LIFE AND VISION

Frances Spalding

Frances Spalding

National Portrait Gallery, London

CONTENTS

Three Guineas

Virginia Woolf

DIRECTOR'S FOREWORD

Not a single educated man's daughter, Whitaker [the Almanack*] says, is thought capable of teaching the literature of her own language at either university. Nor is her opinion worth asking … when it comes to buying a picture for the National Gallery, a portrait for the Portrait Gallery, or a mummy for the British Museum. How can it be worth your while to ask us to protect culture and intellectual liberty when, as Whitaker proves with his cold facts, you have no belief that our advice is worth having …?*

Virginia Woolf, *Three Guineas*, 1938, pp.100–1

Three Guineas by Virginia Woolf, Hogarth Press, 1938. Cover design by Vanessa Bell.

Making an exhibition about Virginia Woolf would always be a complex enterprise. Woolf's widely acknowledged significance at the heart of modernism, the multi-faceted nature of her work as a novelist, essayist, critic and caustic commentator, and the great extent of the secondary literature on her work have all made this exhibition a hugely worthwhile but challenging project. Although Woolf commented, 'We do not know our own souls. Let alone the souls of others,' we are still captivated by trying to discover the essential spirit alongside the biographical narrative of an important thinker. And while an exhibition cannot encapsulate a person, it can aim to connect images, objects and ideas, and to offer an imaginative rendering of them. Our guest curator, Frances Spalding, has risen brilliantly to the challenge by giving viewers and readers a fascinating route through Woolf's life, work and imagery.

The exhibition follows on from various National Portrait Gallery literary exhibitions that have combined portraiture with biography, including the presentation

Virginia Stephen photographed by George Charles Beresford, July 1902. Beresford was the first photographer to play up the sitter's fine profile. Five known photographs remain from this sitting, one of which – belonging to Violet Dickinson and preserved in the two-volume collection of letters she gave to Virginia Woolf (page 56) – shows her face from the other side.

of the Sitwell family in 1994 and the examination of Lord Byron in 2002. Despite having a life cruelly affected by mental instability and illness, Virginia Woolf was crucially determined to overthrow the constraints of her Victorian upbringing and establish new forms of creative writing and criticism. As Spalding puts it, Woolf 'wonders what will happen to the novel if writers do with words what the Post-Impressionists did with paint'. Roger Fry, organiser of the influential Post-Impressionist exhibitions in London, himself said of Woolf's short stories: 'You're the only one now that Henry James has gone who uses language as a medium of art, who makes the very texture of the words have a meaning and a quality really almost apart from what you are talking about.'

Frances Spalding has researched, structured and selected the exhibition (and this publication), and I am hugely grateful to her for responding so creatively to the enormous task of fitting Woolf's life and achievements into the modest confines of the Gallery's walls and these pages. I am also very grateful to Flora Fricker, Exhibitions Manager, Rosie Wilson, Head of Exhibitions, and Paul Moorhouse, Curator of Twentieth-Century Portraits, for excellent development and management work, and to Calum Storrie for leading the creative design. I should also like to acknowledge warmly Pim Baxter, Natalia Calvocoressi, Rob Carr-Archer, Andrea Easey, Neil Evans, Claire Jackson, Ruth Müller-Wirth, Terence Pepper, Andrew Roff, Nicola Saunders, Jude Simmons, Fiona Smith, Liz Smith, Christopher Tinker, Sarah Tinsley, Denise Vogelsang, Ulrike Wachsmann and Helen Whiteoak, and all the other National Portrait Gallery staff who have contributed to both exhibition and publication. The exhibition has been researched with the assistance of Claudia Tobin, and we have been encouraged by a number of key experts, including Dame Hermione Lee and Richard Shone, and I offer special thanks to them. I would also like to thank the T.S. Eliot Estate for their support of this exhibition.

Finally, very particular thanks go to all those private and public owners of paintings, drawings, photographs and manuscripts, who have so generously lent to the exhibition and made it possible to admire Virginia Woolf in this special visual form.

Sandy Nairne
Director
National Portrait Gallery, London

PROLOGUE

In October 1940 the Bloomsbury house in which Virginia Woolf wrote a great many of her novels was hit by a bomb. As it happened, she and her husband Leonard had the previous year moved out of 52 Tavistock Square, owing to the disturbance caused by demolition work in preparation for a large new hotel. Although their lease on this house ran until 1941 and they still had to pay rent, they had moved a short distance in August 1939 to 37 Mecklenburgh Square.

At Tavistock Square, which they hoped to sub-let, they left behind a set of decorative wall panels that Virginia Woolf had commissioned from Vanessa Bell and Duncan Grant for a third-floor sitting-room. The success of this scheme had led to it being illustrated in *Vogue* magazine (overleaf). This was the room in which the Woolfs received many guests, and where Virginia was photographed in June 1939, shortly before the move to Mecklenburgh Square, by the expatriate German living in France, Gisèle Freund. It was the last sitting she gave to a professional photographer.

Freund, who was closely associated in Paris with Sylvia Beach, her bookshop Shakespeare & Company, and its visiting authors, including James Joyce, specialised in photographs of writers. Indeed, it was Joyce who suggested that she should add to her collection by going to London. He assured her that if English writers knew she had photographed him and that he was pleased with the results, they would readily agree to sit for her. This proved correct, and she successfully photographed T.S. Eliot, Elizabeth Bowen, George Bernard Shaw, Vita Sackville-West, who also provided her with a letter of introduction, Herbert Read and Peggy Guggenheim, Victoria Ocampo and Hugh Walpole.

Virginia Woolf, vintage print of photograph by Gisèle Freund in the third-floor sitting-room at 52 Tavistock Square, 24 June 1939.

13

Panels by Duncan Grant and Vanessa Bell in Mrs. Woolf's house in Tavistock Square. The walls are pale dove-grey, the panels glossy white with tomato-red borders and oval "fonds" alternately in sienna pink and maple yellow. The subjects are painted in umbers, browns, and white, with touches of lettuce-green. The narrow frieze is in wallpaper with "écriture," of subdued violet on white and lemon yellow

MODERN ENGLISH DECORATION

Some Examples of the Interesting Work

Of Duncan Grant and Vanessa Bell

Three panels in detail, from the room illustrated above

FOR some time past "period" rooms have been the fashion. First it was the picturesque Elizabethan and Jacobean, then Queen Anne, the eighteenth century, the Regency, the French "Empire," and even, latterly, the Victorian. Very charming such rooms can be, with their pleasant literary associations, their slight air of "pose." But, necessarily, they are a little artificial, in that they are the products of a bygone age, whose thoughts, whose aspirations, whose whole life was totally different from ours. But is there any reason why we should not consider our own day as a "period"—the only period for us which is not in some sense artificial—and set aside at any rate one room in our own house which shall be truly representative of the best in it ? It is not as if this were an age devoid of artistic effort ; on the contrary, there is at present in this country an artistic activity which is producing work more interesting and more vital than anything that has made its appearance here during the last hundred years. Moreover,

many of the leading artists in this modern movement (which is derived largely from Cézanne and the French Impressionists, though it must not for a moment be supposed, as some critics have suggested, that it despises the Old Masters) have turned their attention to decorative work.

Among these are Duncan Grant and Vanessa Bell, who even before the war were associated with a group of artists who produced work of this kind under the leadership of Roger Fry. The war, unfortunately, put a complete stop to this enterprise, but not before they had produced a great many charming things in the way of furniture, stuffs, and pottery, practical as well as beautiful. The individual practical aspect of each object is one of the things to which the artist decorator pays the greatest attention. In the useful arts, beauty and usefulness are interdependent, and mere ornament which hinders practical use is, *ipso facto*, inartistic.

The illustrations to this article are all taken from decorative work done by Duncan Grant

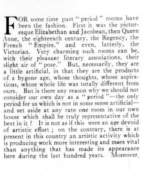

Virginia Woolf, however, initially turned her down. That is, until Victoria Ocampo, the wealthy Argentinian founder and publisher of the literary review *Sur*, whom Woolf admired, turned up at Tavistock Square with Freund in tow in order to show Woolf contact sheets of the literary men and women Freund had photographed. Under pressure, Woolf gave in, and a sitting was arranged for later that same day. Woolf's diary, written before the afternoon session commenced, reveals much irritation: 'No getting out of it, with Okampo [*sic*] on the sofa, & Freund there in the flesh. So my afternoon is gone in the way to me most detestable and upsetting of all.' Freund had recently begun working with colour film, which had just come on to the market, and Woolf dreaded becoming a 'life-sized life coloured animated photograph', yet it pleased her that, at her request, Leonard would also be photographed.[1]

She left no account of this sitting, but we can deduce, from details supplied by Freund and from other clues, that it was an unexpected success. Perhaps Woolf's dread was removed by Joyce's message, or Vita Sackville-West's introductory letter, for the photographs show that she willingly collaborated: in fact, she offered to show Freund her wardrobe so that she could help choose the most suitable clothes, and three times changed her blouse and once the jacket she was wearing. At one point she proudly informed Freund that there had been a celebrated photographer in her own family, and she brought out a copy of the book that the Hogarth Press had published of Julia Margaret Cameron's photographs, with essays by herself and Roger Fry, and this she inscribed to Freund.

Out of this session came some of the most eloquent photo-portraits of Woolf ever produced. They vary in mood, as outward composure gives way to melancholy introspection. They are also the only colour photographs of Woolf ever taken. For technical reasons, it was not possible to publish them in colour at the time, and for many years they were known only in black-and-white format. But in colour they gain additional interest, not least because they provide the only record in existence of the tones and hues used in the decorative scheme for the third-floor sitting-room at 52 Tavistock Square. After a bomb had sliced open the house in October 1940, and destroyed the better part of this room, the decorations on the fireplace wall could be seen from the street below, a fragile reminder of a different age, a different way of life.

The Woolfs received the news that 52 Tavistock Square had been destroyed while in Sussex. Although 37 Mecklenburgh Square had not received a direct hit, it too had suffered from the bombing. On 17 October, the Woolfs drove to London to assess the damage. One of the first things Woolf saw on arriving in Bloomsbury was a queue, mostly of children with suitcases, outside Warren Street Tube station, waiting for shelter from the night raids. Her diary records:

'Modern English Decoration', early November, 1924, an article in *Vogue* magazine on the decorative work of Duncan Grant and Vanessa Bell, showing, on this opening page, the Woolfs' sitting-room at 52 Tavistock Square.

Gisèle Freund

So to Tavistock Sq. With a sigh of relief saw a heap of ruins. Three houses, I shd. say gone. Basement all rubble. Only relics an old basket chair (bought in Fitzroy Square days) & Penmans board To Let. Otherwise bricks & wood splinters. One glass door in the next house hanging. I cd just see a piece of my studio wall standing: otherwise rubble where I wrote so many books. Open air where we sat so many nights, gave so many parties …. So to Mec[klenburgh Square]. All again litter, glass, black soft dust, plaster powder …. Books all over the dining room floor. In my sitting room glass all over Mrs Hunter's cabinet – & so on. Only the drawing room with windows almost whole. A wind blowing through. I began to hunt out diaries. What cd we salvage in this little car? Darwin, & the Silver, and some glass and china …[2]

Sunday Oct. 20th

By this date, Woolf's habit of keeping a diary had filled over thirty notebooks. These she found amid the broken glass, dust and litter, and took them away to the relative safety of their cottage at Rodmell. After her death, they were moved for safe keeping to the vault of Westminster Bank in Lewes, where they lay silent for many years. Had they been destroyed, as was so nearly the case, we would know far less today about Virginia Woolf, not just about the facts of her life, but also about her creativity and the period in which she lived, for she had occupied a position that brought her close to the centre of English political, cultural and social life.

These diaries first came to public attention in 1953, when Leonard Woolf selected passages from them for *A Writer's Diary*. He then made them available to his nephew Quentin Bell, who had been appointed the official biographer of Virginia Woolf; and afterwards the diaries were edited, with a sharp eye to 'accuracy/relevance/ concision/interest', by Quentin's wife Anne Olivier Bell, in five volumes, and published by the Hogarth Press between 1977 and 1984.[3] 'We are offered', Olivier Bell writes of these diaries, 'an enlightened and privileged view not so much of a group as of English history unfolding.'[4] The story of these phoenix-like diaries justifies the claim that Virginia Woolf once made on the radio, when she argued that words survive the chops and changes of time almost better than any other substance.

Above, left: Original watercolour sketch by Vanessa Bell for dust jacket of *A Writer's Diary*, n.d.

Above, right: The final design was turned upside down. Published by the Hogarth Press in 1953.

19

At one moment, in the New York Public Library, while researching this Virginia Woolf exhibition, I stood beside a photocopying machine with a library assistant. While we waited for it to perform, he mentioned that he had recently read *The Waves*, Woolf's most experimental novel. He had not taken to it at first, he admitted, but by the end had been shaken and astonished by the depth of her empathetic reach. His experience must be similar to that of countless others, for Woolf's writings have reached across the more usual cultural divides of gender, class, education, race and nationality, thereby altering and enriching millions of lives. There are nowadays many accounts of Woolf's own life, while scholarship on her work is myriad. It has been admired, imitated, analysed, critiqued, deconstructed, satirised, appropriated and contested. It continues to inspire contemporary authors and has been adapted for both stage and screen. Where does this exhibition fit in such a crowded field?

It offers, for those either familiar or unfamiliar with Virginia Woolf, a visual narrative akin to a portrait. As with all portraits, it is necessarily selective. It looks at telling ingredients in each period of her life; catches the alterations in her dress and appearance, and in her face, which has since gathered such public resonance and iconicity. It gathers in some of her family, friends, rivals and associates; it

The Diary of Virginia Woolf, Volume III, 1925–1930, Hogarth Press, 1980. One of the five volumes that comprise the edited version of her diary. Cover design by Duncan Grant.

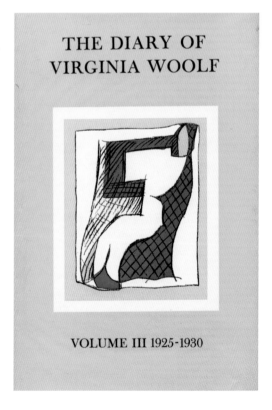

THE DIARY OF VIRGINIA WOOLF

VOLUME III 1925-1930

touches also on her creative ambitions, interests and ideas, drawing attention to things well known as well as others that are less well known. It also contains some items that have never before been put on public view.

Portraiture and the fixing of identity figured largely in her life. She grew up surrounded by Julia Margaret Cameron's photographs of her female relatives and famous men, and also painted and drawn portraits by the great Victorian artist G.F. Watts. Her father was a trustee of the National Portrait Gallery and the editor of the first twenty-six volumes of *The Dictionary of National Biography*. Woolf herself wrote a biography of Roger Fry and readily composed memorable vignettes of people she knew or met. In turn, she sat for her own portrait to artists and photographers on many occasions. Yet in her own work she was driven by a desire to go beneath the surface, to unfix appearances, and to acknowledge uncertainty and the unfinished. Above all, she recognised the play of selves within us, and the conundrum this presents to the modernist writer or painter when confronted with the need to register character or appearance.

Woolf not only challenged the traditions governing the shape and purpose of the novel, she also wrote two major political works, enough essays and reviews to fill six fat volumes, thousands of letters, and a diary that sits alongside the greatest in this genre. She was, in addition, an intensely observant writer who shook out information, meanings and experience from things seen. This is another reason why an exhibition is an appropriate vehicle through which to hint at the formation of her vision. As her fame grew, her visibility increased, as did her awareness of the need for self-presentation. In the course of this exhibition, portraits in various media track the mutations in her appearance. They also mark the various stages in her life, as she emerges from her Victorian background, becomes associated with Bloomsbury, labours for the Hogarth Press and its authors, embarks on her own radical literary endeavours, and then permits the emergence of her political self, while responding also to the pressures of the historical moment. Along the way, she did much to reveal the fluidity between the public sphere and the private self, between the seen and the unseen, between the concealed as well as the outwardly stated. 'One can only believe entirely,' she writes teasingly in *Orlando*, 'in what one cannot see.'

NOTES

1   *The Diary of Virginia Woolf, Vol. 5: 1936–1941*, ed. Anne Olivier Bell (Hogarth Press, London, 1984), p.220.

2   Ibid., pp.330–1.

3   Those four words – accuracy, relevance, concision and interest – were Olivier Bell's objectives when writing the annotations to the text and were pinned up before her desk. See Anne Olivier Bell, *Editing Virginia Woolf's Diary* (The Bloomsbury Workshop, London, 1990), p.22.

4   *The Diary of Virginia Woolf, Vol. 5*, p.x.

1 'WHO WAS I THEN?'

'Who was I then?' Virginia Woolf asked this question, in the way that many do when they look back on their earlier life. The date was 18 April 1939, and she had decided to take time off from work on her biography of Roger Fry in order to write an autobiographical memoir. Surprisingly, for the darkening situation in Europe made her angry and despondent, her essay is light and discursive. It is titled 'A Sketch of the Past', and each section begins with a few details about her present life so as to create a platform from which to look back at the past. Written to be read aloud to her friends within Bloomsbury's Memoir Club (overleaf), it was not published in her lifetime. Eventually it formed part of *Moments of Being*, a collection of autobiographical writings that slowly came to be regarded as indispensable to the study of Woolf's life and fiction.[1]

Woolf's question is intriguing, as she did much to trouble the notion of a core self and to show its mutability. Yet in 'A Sketch of the Past' she proceeds to offer exact and explicit details about her family's ancestry, class and social context. Even so, Virginia Woolf scholars discern in this essay gaps, deferrals, displacement and anger.

The question asked in 'A Sketch of the Past' takes us straight into the Victorian world of her childhood.

> Who was I then? Adeline Virginia Stephen, the second daughter of Leslie and Julia Prinsep Stephen, born on 25th January 1882, descended from a great many people, some famous, others obscure; born not of rich parents but of well-to-do parents, born into a very communicative, literate letter-writing, visiting, articulate, late nineteenth-century world …[2]

Vanessa Stephen painting, with Virginia seated beside her, and (left to right) Thoby and Adrian behind. Photographed by Stella Duckworth, *c.*1896.

The Memoir Club by Vanessa Bell, *c.*1943. The Memoir Club, founded in 1920, met at intervals over many years, renewing the bonds of friendship within Bloomsbury. Those shown here, from left to right, include Duncan Grant, Leonard Woolf, Vanessa Bell, Clive Bell, David Garnett, Maynard and Lydia Keynes, Desmond and Molly MacCarthy, Quentin Bell and E.M. Forster. Three deceased members – Virginia Woolf, Lytton Strachey and Roger Fry – are represented on the wall behind.

The niche here described is that of the professional upper-middle class, but Woolf's family also belonged to what the historian Noel Annan identified as 'the intellectual aristocracy'.[3] This he associated with a network of families and intellectual dynasties whose power rested not primarily on hereditary rights or wealth, but on knowledge, mental agility and a shared emotional climate. This status group was first propelled to power in the 1850s and 1860s and reached a pre-eminent position in the 1870s.

Woolf's choice of adjectives in the above passage – 'communicative … literate … articulate' – affirms the importance of speech, books and ideas in the family home. In one photograph taken in 1893, she sits in the background, watching her parents read. In this home environment words mattered, had weight and influence; and channels of communication were kept open, even when distorted by grief. Woolf's mother and maternal grandmother, Julia Stephen and Maria Jackson (née Pattle), wrote daily letters to each other because the habit of letter-writing was ingrained. A great many letters were tied up in bundles and kept, for the past was valued and preserved.

The critical commentary on Woolf's relationship with her father has been weighted towards the last seven years of his life when, twice widowed, he became irascible, irrational, mawkish and self-obsessed. But, prior to this, his formative influence on Virginia Stephen had been immediate and far-reaching. 'My impression as a child always was that my father was not very much older than we were,' Woolf writes, instancing the way he would sail boats with his children on the Round Pond in Kensington Gardens, also recalling how one of these boats had

Julia and Leslie Stephen reading at Talland House, watched by their daughter, Virginia. Photographed by Vanessa Stephen, 1893.

been fitted out by him with mast and sails in the style of a Cornish lugger. At this stage their relationship was one of 'perfectly equal companionship'.[4] Leslie also gifted Virginia with fiction, poetry and books. As soon as his children were old enough, he read aloud to them for an hour and a half every evening in the drawing room. After working his way through some children's classics, he went through all thirty-two of Sir Walter Scott's Waverley novels. He knew a vast store of English poetry by heart and, lying back in his chair and shutting his eyes, would recite. 'Thus,' his daughter wrote, 'many of the great English poems now seem to me inseparable from my father; I hear in them not only his voice, but in some sort his teaching and belief.'[5]

LITTLE HOLLAND HOUSE

One childhood memory identified in 'A Sketch of the Past' concerned her mother, who, while they were out walking one day, suddenly darted forward and with a clap of her hands announced, 'That was where it was!' For a moment the past was more visible than the present, for she was pointing to the site where Little Holland House had stood and where she had spent a part of her childhood.[6] This house

27

and all those associated with it haunted Virginia Woolf, even though she never saw it, for it was demolished in 1875, seven years before she was born. The anecdotes it engendered became part of her family history. They evoked the romance of the past; they quickened her sense of the absurd; and later they gave her a subject for affectionate social satire.

A lease on this house had been taken in 1850 by Thoby Prinsep, a director of the East India Company and a Persian scholar, whose wife Sarah, like Woolf's grandmother Maria Jackson, was one of the Pattle sisters, renowned for their beauty. Their mother had been a French aristocrat, and much of their childhood had been spent in France; the unorthodox education they received had largely been acquired while staying with their French grandmother in Versailles. There were seven sisters in total, and all were exceptionally beautiful, aside from Julia

Alfred Tennyson, 1st Baron Tennyson photographed by Julia Margaret Cameron, 1869. Virginia Woolf respected and admired this great Victorian but also found in him comic potential.

Margaret, who was notably plain and shorter than the rest, and in middle age became rather stout. Her marriage to Charles Cameron, the first lawyer on India's Supreme Council, took her to Calcutta, where she became a dominant force within its European society. Later in life, after their return to England, Julia Margaret Cameron took up photography, then a complicated, slow and onerous medium that often left her reeking of chemicals. Despite that and the despotic manner she had acquired in the colonies, she managed to dragoon the great and the good, friends, relatives, servants or even complete strangers into posing for her. If they tried to refuse, she clenched her fists and spoke of eternal damnation.

Many of her sitters she first encountered at Little Holland House. It was sur-rounded by an ample garden and mature trees, for it had been built when Kensington was on the very edge of London. In summer the Prinseps' guests spilled on to the lawn, and among them might be famous names of the day – Prime Minister William Gladstone, the critic John Ruskin, the painter Sir Edward Burne-Jones, the astronomer Sir William Herschel, and the poets Alfred, Lord Tennyson and Robert Browning, to name just a few. The Pattle sisters were a major draw. With their high spirits, generosity and unconventional ways, they created a relaxed, slightly bohemian atmosphere. But behind this lay considerable power, hence the term coined by the dramatist Sir Henry Taylor, 'Pattledom'.[7] The sisters were great admirers of talent; they took Burne-Jones in when he was ill and gave the artist G.F. Watts a quaint set of rooms on the upper floor. He intended to stay a week, but remained in residence for twenty-one years; and even when he married, he did not move out. His wife, a brilliant young actress, had initially arrived at Little Holland House as his model, her gestures and poses perfectly matching his needs. Ellen Terry was then seventeen, Watts, forty-seven. He married her, he said, to save her from degradation. More importantly, Mrs Prinsep wished it.

It was, of course, a disastrous match. Watts was old for his age, tetchy and impatient, and almost permanently wore galoshes to protect himself from the damp. Ellen was impetuous and immature. Outside the studio, this future actress had no real role at Little Holland House and was advised to keep silent in company. She protested by sliding down the banisters, shaking out her hairpins at teatime so that her hair fell down, and then appeared at one of the Prinseps' dinner parties as Cupid, wearing a pair of pink tights. Some say she eloped with another man, others suggest she was ignominiously sent home: the marriage, such as it was, had lasted less than a year.

George Frederic and Mary Watts at the second Little Holland House photographed by Frederick Hollyer, 1887. Watts built the house for himself after the first one had been demolished.

31

Virginia Woolf later put Mrs Cameron, Watts and Ellen Terry into her burlesque *Freshwater* (named after Freshwater on the Isle of Wight, where Tennyson lived), written to be performed by family and friends in the London studio of her sister Vanessa Bell.[8] In the play Watts is struggling to paint the toes on his figure of Mammon. 'Signor', as he was called at Little Holland House, was often teased by the Pattle sisters for being in a 'high-art' mood. He shrugged off his failed marriage and went on to garner fame, wealth and prestige. As the demise of Little Holland House approached, he commissioned C.R. Cockerell to build a house for himself around the corner, in Melbury Road, and also called it Little Holland House. Virginia Woolf recollected visits to this house on Sunday mornings with her mother, for Watts had painted portraits of her parents and always remained a close family friend. His pencil drawing of Maria Jackson sat on the corner of her daughter's desk, whether the family was in London or Cornwall, for Julia took it with her. One of Virginia's childhood letters was written from Limnerslease, the house in the country, outside Guildford in Surrey, that Watts had built after he married again, at the age of sixty-nine. By then he had portrayed many leading Victorians. He was still painting elaborate allegories, such as *Time, Death and Judgement* (previous page), which strained after philosophical and moral meanings, rather like the figures on the ceiling of the Sistine Chapel in Rome. He had in fact become 'England's Michelangelo', for in the late Victorian period his reputation seemed unassailable.

In this rich cultural environment the young Virginia Stephen would have been aware of the desire to fix facts and to achieve certainty. At home in 22 Hyde Park Gate, each time they heard a sudden thud, the children in the nursery knew that a book had fallen to the floor from their father's lap as he sat writing in his rocking chair in the room above. An eminent literary critic, Leslie Stephen was capable of producing an 8,000-word article at one sitting. The author of many books, including *The History of English Thought in the Eighteenth Century* in two volumes, he also dedicated time and energy to editing the first twenty-six volumes of *The Dictionary of National Biography*.[9] In their different ways he and Watts strove to put in place for posterity verbal and visual narratives about identity that would have enduring authority. The assumptions that shored up their endeavour were those against which a younger generation would rebel.

EARLY INFLUENCES

Leslie Stephen had spent ten years of his life as a don at Cambridge University, and it had sharpened his honesty, integrity and intellect. Virginia Woolf did not particularly like Cambridge intellectuals, for she found them lacking in 'picturesqueness, oddity, romance',[10] but association with her father made her familiar with the Cambridge intellectual yardstick, which she applied to other types, such as the diplomat and writer Harold Nicolson and the novelist Hugh Walpole. They did not measure up, and she found herself saying inwardly, 'how you miss the mark,

here and here and here',[11] while at the same time being amused and stimulated by their presence, for they were more colourful than most Cambridge intellectuals. As the young Virginia Stephen, she had become familiar with her father's 'clear, strong intellect'[12] and the way it removed clutter, falsity and superstition. In one of her childhood letters, sent to her mother from Limnerslease, she mentions that Mrs Watts had gone to church at half past seven in the morning. This might have surprised her, for the habit of church-going was not part of the Stephen family routine, despite the fact that Leslie Stephen, while at Trinity Hall, Cambridge, had accepted a fellowship that committed him to taking orders, which he had done. But eventually his family background – he was descended from a long line of energetic, argumentative, professional men who had left their mark on intellectual and legal circles – came to the fore and he began to doubt the Christian religion.

When I ceased to accept the teaching of my youth, it was not so much a process of giving up beliefs as of discovering that I had never really believed. The contrast between the genuine convictions that guide and govern our conduct, and the professions which we were taught to repeat in church, when once realised, was too glaring. One belonged to the world of realities and the other to the world of dreams.[13]

Leslie Stephen's interest in philosophy, in John Stuart Mill, Thomas Hobbes and the British empiricists, had also played a part; and after reading Auguste Comte, he could no longer declaim the story of the Flood and Noah's ark as if it were sacred truth. Finding himself unable to take part in college services, he resigned his tutorship, at the Master's request, but was allowed to retain his fellowship, and stayed on at Cambridge a couple more years, fulfilling minor duties. Eventually, he decided to make literature his profession, and by January 1865 he was settled in London, which he saw as 'plainly the best place for that profession'.[14] Journalism and books poured out of him, among them *Essays on Free-Thinking and Plain-Speaking* (1873). His thoughts on agnosticism brought him to the attention of a young widow, Julia Duckworth. They did much to confirm her in her own thoughts on the matter of religion.

Both Virginia Woolf's parents had been married before. Julia had been widowed in 1870, at the age of twenty-four, when her first husband, Herbert Duckworth, had reached into a tree to pick a fig and burst an unsuspected abscess. She was then pregnant with their third child, who was born six weeks later. With three young children (George, Stella and Gerald) in her care, she could not give full vent to her pain and grief. She often visited Freshwater in order to stay with her aunt Julia Margaret Cameron, who photographed her extensively. Evidently, they were very close,[15] as it was to the older woman that the younger admitted, after five years of widowhood, that she wished she could die. Leslie Stephen was similarly bereft, having lost his first wife, Minny – Thackeray's daughter Harriet Marian – after eight happy years of marriage. Julia Duckworth knew them both, and happened to visit them on the evening of 27 November 1875. Minny was then pregnant with

their second child. Afterwards, Julia recollected that because their happiness was so pronounced, she had felt like an intruder and soon went home. That same night Minny was taken with convulsions and died the next day. Leslie Stephen never again celebrated his birthday as it was identical with the date of Minny's death.

Julia was on hand to comfort Leslie Stephen and Minny's sister Anny, who was part of the household. In January 1876 she went with them both to Brighton for a rest. She also helped with their move from Southwell Gardens to Hyde Park Gate, where they became her neighbours. When Leslie Stephen first proposed to her, she knew that she returned his love, but doubted whether she had the power in her to start a new life. Over the next year they saw each other daily. In January 1878 she committed herself to him, and in March they married. The self-denial and censoring restraint that had been a necessity in early widowhood had marked her face, bearing and character. Leslie Stephen saw this: himself a pioneering Alpine climber, he likened Julia to his beloved Alps, which, he said, 'make me feel better yet have a touch of melancholy and strictness'.[16] The simile was apt. Looking back on her childhood, Virginia Woolf wrote: 'What my mother was like when she was as happy as anyone can be, I have no notion. Not a sound or scene has survived.'[17] Nevertheless, this same woman moved into Leslie Stephen's house with her three children. At that time Laura, Leslie's daughter by Minny, was also living there,[18] and they were all soon to be joined by four Stephen siblings, Thoby, Vanessa, Virginia and Adrian.

EMINENT VICTORIANS

One ingredient in Virginia Stephen's parental home was a reverence for those who were truly great. This was made visible at Hyde Park Gate by the photographs of eminent Victorians (pages 52–3), most taken by Julia Margaret Cameron, that

Above, left: The Duckworth and Stephen siblings at Alenhoe, 1892, Wimbledon. Back row, left to right: Gerald Duckworth, Virginia, Thoby and Vanessa Stephen and George Duckworth. Front row, left to right: Adrian Stephen, Julia and Leslie Stephen.

Above, right: Virginia and Adrian playing cricket, c.1886. The importance of cricket to the Duckworth-Stephen family in Cornwall is upheld by this and the photograph overleaf.

Vanessa (right) and Virginia playing cricket at St Ives, c.1894.

hung on the walls alongside Watts's paintings and portraits, and the Sir Joshua Reynolds engravings in the dining-room; and it was further evidenced by Leslie Stephen's short biographies of Samuel Johnson, Alexander Pope, Jonathan Swift, George Eliot and Hobbes, which he wrote for the 'English Men of Letters' series. This attitude towards great men and women had been boosted by one of their circle, Thomas Carlyle, whose *On Heroes, Hero-Worship, and the Heroic in History* had first been published in 1841. In 1895, some fourteen years after Carlyle's death, his house – number 5 (now 24) Cheyne Walk in Chelsea – became London's first literary shrine. Leslie Stephen had been a key figure behind this move. The family newspaper, the *Hyde Park Gate News*, written by the Stephen children, records how they accompanied him to the Mansion House, the office of the Lord Mayor of London, to a meeting concerning the future of Carlyle's house.[19] Another particular favourite of Leslie Stephen was the naturalist Charles Darwin. 'He was in town for a few days,' Stephen wrote to another friend, 'and most kindly called upon me. You may believe that I was proud to welcome him, for of all eminent men that I have ever seen he is beyond comparison the most attractive to me. There is something almost pathetic in his simplicity and friendliness.'[20]

In 'A Sketch of the Past', Virginia Woolf recollected that she too caught the habit and mentally genuflected to greatness in others. Of her childhood, she wrote:

> Great men stood in the background. Meredith, Henry James, Watts, Burne-Jones, Sidgwick, Haldane, Morley …. I remember still more clearly the great ceremony of our visits to great men. For father and mother were equally respectful of greatness. And the honour and privilege of our position impressed themselves on us. I remember Meredith dropping slices of lemon into his tea. I remember that Watts had great bowls of whipped cream; and a plate of minced meat …. He wore ruffles at his wrists and a long grey dressing gown. And we went to Little Holland House always on a Sunday morning …. I remember Meredith's growl; and I remember the hesitations and adumbrations with which Henry James made the drawing room seem rich and dusky. Greatness still seems to me a positive possession; booming; eccentric; set apart; something to which I am led up dutifully by my parents. It is a bodily presence; it has nothing to do with anything said. It exists in certain people. But it never exists now. I cannot remember ever to have felt greatness since I was a child.[21]

This family tradition is guyed in her second novel *Night and Day* (1919). 'It was a Sunday evening in October,' the book begins, 'and in common with many other young ladies of her class, Katherine Hilbery was pouring out tea.' To her mother's tea party comes a young man, Ralph Denham. Instructed by her mother to show Denham the shrine-like room filled with memorabilia of her grandfather, the famous poet Richard Alardyce, Katherine embarks on this duty and, while Denham examines a manuscript, finds herself glancing up at a portrait of her grandfather. 'That magnificent ghostly head on the canvas, surely, never beheld all the trivialities of a Sunday afternoon, and it did not seem to matter what she and this young man said to each other, for they were only small people.' Yet the conversation, as it unfolds, is made interesting and awkward by Denham's antagonism to Katherine's class, and eventually his protest is voiced. '"You'll never know anything at first hand," he began, almost savagely. "It's all been done for you. You'll never know the pleasure of buying things after saving up for them, or reading books for the first time, or making discoveries."' Worse is to come when he bursts out: '"I hate great men. The worship of greatness in the nineteenth century seems to me to explain the worthlessness of that generation."' Katherine draws breath, as if about to make a vigorous reply, but the shutting of a door distracts them.[22]

The Hyde Park Gate News No. 8, Vol. V, 25 February 1895. A family newspaper by the Stephen children. The opening topic of this issue describes a meeting held at the Mansion House, in connection with the move, strongly supported by Leslie Stephen, to preserve for the nation Carlyle's house in Chelsea. It was well attended, and included the Lord Mayor and the Ambassador of the United States.

Hyde Park Gate News.

NO. 8. VOL. V   Monday, February 25th 1895.

On Friday we sent a special correspondent to the Mansion House to report upon the meeting held there for the purpose of buying Carlyle's house in Chelsea. We were ushered into a large room with great pictures of royalty hanging on the walls, and massive chandeliers, and mirrors and gigantic pillars. A great number of people were seated in the room where we had a separate table in the middle just beneath the raised platform where the Lord Mayor and the speakers were going to sit. As we finished our survey of the appartment a butler announced in stalwart tones "His Worship the Lord Mayor, and His Excellency the Ambassador of the United States!" We all rose to our feet, and strained to catch a glimpse of a little gentleman in a very tight frock coat with an enormous diamond star upon his breast who walked into the room followed by selveral other gentleman, and took his place upon an especially magnificent arm chair with the mottoe "Domine. dirige nos" emblazoned upon it. His Worship then rose, and remarked that meetings held at the Mansion House were generally connected with some charitable purpose, or some purpose needing funds. His Worship continued with an eulogy upon Mr Carlyle and his works, and ended with the following magnificent remark, which we believe partly caused the Lady Mayoress to jump from her chair with delight. "I have just come from a meeting when Lord —— (inaudible) one of Eylands greatest soldiers, who, I may remark, was not more distinguished in his field of battle than Carlyle was in his field of letters (cheers, hear hear) Mr Stevens then read rather a confused account of his financial affairs, and then the Lord Mayor called upon the Marquis of Ripon for his speech. The Marquis is a small man, with a long beard, and

This awkward scene in *Night and Day* draws on Virginia Woolf's memories of life at Hyde Park Gate, and on her experience of visiting Carlyle's preserved house.[23] The weight of the past in London may explain why Cornwall, to which the family escaped in the summer months, remained luminescent in Woolf's memory. The year before Virginia was born, Leslie Stephen had taken a lease, as he told a friend, on 'a little house at St Ives, down at the very toe-nail of England', which brought the advantage that 'the children will be able to run straight out of the house to a lovely bit of sand and have good air and quiet'.[24] Talland House, as it was called, became their summer home for the next twelve years (overleaf). This involved the removal from London to St Ives of a large part of the household – cook, servants, dogs, children and parents, as well as numerous trunks, boxes and bags. They would stay three to four months. Greatness followed them here too, in the form of Henry James (page 41), who was one of their many visitors. (Another guest, M.R. James, the Cambridge don and writer of ghost stories, found himself so strongly attracted to Stella Duckworth that he left early, much to his mother's relief, as she was dreading the thought of him marrying into this agnostic family.)

St Ives fishermen hauling in pilchards by means of a seine net, 1894.

The Stephen family's summer retreat, Talland House in St Ives, Cornwall, c.1882–94.

It may have been en route to St Ives that Virginia acquired her first memory: of red and purple flowers on a black ground – her mother's dress. But the most important of all her early memories, she insisted, was associated with the night nursery where she had heard the waves breaking and unfurling on the beach, while the blind, blown in by the wind, dragged its little acorn across the floor. 'If life has a base that it stands on, if it is a bowl that one fills and fills and fills – then my bowl without any doubt stands upon this memory.'[25]

Left: Adrian and Julia
Stephen with Henry James,
seated on the steps, 1894.

Below: Julia Stephen and
her youngest child, Adrian,
1886.

'The sea blazed gold.' This short sentence delivers the climax in the opening section of Woolf's 1931 novel *The Waves*. This passage, using terse description and near-abstract language, in a manner similar to a Post-Impressionist painting, evokes the steady advance of light as the day begins and the sun rises. Memories of holidays on the Cornish coast not only punctuate this novel, but also open *Jacob's Room*, and flood through *To the Lighthouse*, even though it is ostensibly set in Scotland. In this last novel the eponymous lighthouse recalls the Godrevy light-house at St Ives, which Virginia Stephen could have viewed from the house. The importance of this coastline and all it gave her cannot be overemphasised. Even in adulthood, after the house had been given up, she made ten return visits to it between 1905 and 1919.

The reason Leslie Stephen sold the house was that he could not bear to revisit it after Julia's death. She died young, at the age of forty-nine, worn out, it is said, by her selfless dedication to the needs of others. Photographs of her in later life show her looking much older than her actual age. When Woolf came to write about Mrs Pargiter's final illness in her novel *The Years* some forty years later, she drew on her memory of the tense waiting that undermined normality, as the Stephen family tried to continue with everyday life while their mother gradually declined. Soon after Julia's death in 1895, Virginia had her first breakdown.

FIRST BREAKDOWN

There is scant record of this breakdown other than the brief notes found in her half-sister Stella Duckworth's appointment diaries. The entry for 13 October 1896 reads: 'Took Ginia to [Dr] Seton & he says she must do less lessons & be very careful not to exert herself – her pulse 146. Father in a great state. We are to see Seton again in a week.' Eight days later, on 21 October, the prognosis is more severe: 'To Seton with Ginia. He says she must give up lessons entirely till January & must be out 4 hours a day. Is to go and see him again in 4 weeks time.' Stella, who had done much to assist with the Stephen children when they were small and who had always been close to her mother, immediately replaced Julia as the maternal figure in Virginia's life. But this period brims with tragedy, owing to Stella's untimely death in 1897, only a few months after her marriage to Jack Hills. Woolf herself is the most useful source on her own state during these fateful years.

My mother's death fell into the very middle of that amorphous time. That made it much more broken. The whole thing was strained. This brought on, naturally, my first 'breakdown'. It was found that I had a pulse that raced. It beat so quickly that I could hardly bear it. No lessons, no excitement: open air, simple life. So I lived the two years between my mother's death and Stella's in a state of physical distress … I was terrified of people – used to turn red if spoken to. Used to sit up in my room raging – at father, at George, and read and read and read. But I never wrote. For two years I never wrote.[26]

She recovered mentally, but the six years between 1898 and 1904 remain a muffled, repressed period in her life. The family still took holidays in parts of the country other than Cornwall, and her habit of taking walks, in both town or countryside, was a source of solace. Yet 22 Hyde Park Gate, with its heavy colours and lack of light, had become for her a 'cage'.[27] Leslie Stephen vented his rage at being twice widowed on his elder daughter Vanessa. Now responsible for the running of the house, she was obliged to present him each week with the account book listing expenditures. It produced a torrid drama: he groaned, he shouted, expressed horror, anger, self-pity and declared that her extravagance would be the downfall of the family, a claim wholly unsupported by his financial reserves. That a man of such intellect and lovableness had been reduced to this brutal, false and pathetic behaviour left Virginia, the onlooker, with her strong affinity to her father, speechless. 'Never have I felt such rage and such frustration. For not a word of what I felt – that unbounded contempt for him and of pity for Nessa – could be expressed.'[28]

A further cause of anger was her half-brother George Duckworth. A photograph of her and George together conveys something of her abject state, if only through

Stella Duckworth, *c.*1897.

momentary body language. This was the half-brother who had been a hero to the Stephen children in their childhood, who played with them and taught them how to hold their cricket bats straight. Woolf later surmised that his 'profuse, voluble affections' had been held in check by their mother, but after Julia died 'some restraint broke'.[29] Woolf's description of his petting and fondling of her, and her reference to George's 'malefactions', suggests that his attentions breached some code of conduct. Whether this was damaging or not, there is no evidence of sexual abuse. Woolf always retained a degree of affection towards George, and he, in turn, became an admirer of her writing.[30]

More harmful, perhaps, to her sense of self was George's sustained attack on her failure to match up with his idea as to how a young lady of her class should dress and behave. Of her father, Woolf wrote: 'no one was less snobbish than he, no one cared less for rank or luxury'.[31] But George, who was private secretary to the statesman Austen Chamberlain (brother of Prime Minister Neville Chamberlain) and socially much in demand, was very different. Woolf's 'frock-consciousness', which will surface again later, owes much to George Duckworth, who was determined that Virginia, like Vanessa, should now take her place in Victorian upper-middle-class society. This meant changing at a certain point every day into evening dress. A £50 dress allowance, though equivalent to what a live-in maid might be paid for a year's work, was not enough to make a young woman of this class presentable, as Woolf recalls:

A home dress, made by Jane Bride, could be had for a pound or two; but a party dress, made by Mrs Young, cost fifteen guineas. The home dress therefore might be, as on one night that comes back to mind, made cheaply but eccentrically, of a green fabric, bought at Story's the furniture shop. It was not velvet; nor plush; something betwixt and between; and for chairs, presumably, not dresses. Down I came one winter's evening about 1900 in my green dress…. All the lights were turned up in the drawing-room; and by the blazing fire George sat, in dinner jacket and black tie, cuddling the dachshund Schuster, on his knee. He at once fixed on me that extraordinarily observant scrutiny with which he always inspected our clothes. He looked me up and down for a moment as if I were a horse brought into the show ring. Then the sullen look came into his eyes; the look which expressed not simply aesthetic disapproval; but something that went deeper. It was the look of moral, of social, disapproval, as if he scented some kind of insurrection, of defiance of his accepted standards. I knew myself condemned from more points of view than I could then analyse. As I stood there I was conscious of fear; of shame; of something like anguish – a feeling, like so many, out of all proportion to its surface cause. He said at last: 'Go and tear it up.' He spoke in a curiously tart, rasping, peevish voice; the voice of an enraged male; the voice which expressed his serious displeasure at this infringement of a code that meant more to him than he could admit.[32]

George Duckworth and Virginia Stephen, 1897.

45

Monk's House photograph album showing Virginia and Leslie Stephen photographed by George Charles Beresford, 1902.

Leslie Stephen, meanwhile, was losing his strength. He no longer shouted Henry Newbolt's poem 'Admirals All' at the top of his voice as he moved about the house or walked through Kensington Gardens. He still read omnivorously, but he now tired of books before evening and looked forward to light talk at tea-time. 'The tea table', Woolf reminds us, 'rather than the dinner table was the centre of Victorian family life – in our family at least.'[33] She and Vanessa poured out tea and made sure the conversation flowed across the surface of things: a great deal was said about very little. The 'angel of the house' tone of voice, light, gentle, poised and polite, was adopted for these occasions, and it sometimes crept, Woolf later observed angrily, into her essay-writing.

In 1891 Leslie Stephen had resigned from *The Dictionary of National Biography*. Four years later Julia died, and within two weeks Leslie had embarked on a memoir of her and their life together, which inevitably required him to write a fair amount about himself. He wrote and rewrote this memoir, the more finished version filling a fat tome that his children dutifully carried with them through life, housing it under beds and nicknaming it 'The Mausoleum Book'. It had been written primarily for the Stephen and Duckworth children, but publication was not ruled out. His instruction reads: 'I think that the living should settle all things without having their hands tied. Consequently I will not say positively that I forbid you to make any use of this when I am dead.'[34]

He was diagnosed with cancer of the intestine in 1902. That same year he was offered a knighthood, which he thought he should decline because he did not feel such an honour appropriate for a mere 'literary gent', but his family protested and he gave way, putting aside his scruples. He had, after all, been one of the founding fellows of the British Academy, the recipient of four honorary degrees (one from Harvard), a former Trustee of the National Portrait Gallery, and remained a vice-president of the Royal Historical Society. As he remarked in 'The Mausoleum Book', with no small satisfaction, 'I have as many honours as I deserve.' Yet by late autumn 1903, he was too ill to continue with this memoir and the final paragraph is written in Virginia's hand. It reads:

14th Nov. 1903. Dictated to Virginia. I shall write no more in this book. I just note that an operation was performed on me by Sir F. Treves on 12th December 1902. It was considered to be successful, & I improved in strength for two or three months afterwards. Since that time, I have been growing weaker, & I fancy that I shall do no more work. We spent the summer at Netherhampton Salisbury. I am now in bed at 22 Hyde Park Gate. I have only to say to you, my children, that you have all been as good & tender to me as anyone could be during these last months and indeed years. It comforts me to think that you are all so fond of each other that when I am gone you will be the better able to do without me.

He died early the following year, on 22 February 1904.

L. Stephen.   178

L. Stephen.   179

V.S.   L. Stephen   180

NOTES

1   Virginia Woolf, *Moments of Being*, ed. Jeanne Schulkind (Chatto & Windus, London, 1976; Hogarth Press, London, 1985); ed. and rev. Hermione Lee (Pimlico, London, 2002), p.viii. 'A Sketch of the Past' was not included until the 1985 edition. Lee notes in her introduction to the 2002 edition that this essay 'has changed the way her [Woolf's] life story is read, and it throws a strong illuminating light on her fiction'.

2   Virginia Woolf, *Moments of Being*, ed. and rev. Hermione Lee (Pimlico, London, 2002), p.79. Her first name had been chosen in memory of her great aunt Adeline Pattle, who had died the year before her birth.

3   N.G. Annan, 'The Intellectual Aristocracy', in *Studies in Social History*, ed. J.H. Plumb, (Longman, London, 1955), pp.241–87; reprinted in Noel Annan, *The Dons* (HarperCollins, London, 1999), pp.304–41. It has to be acknowledged that the term is controversial. See William Whyte, 'The Intellectual Aristocracy Revisited', *Journal of Victorian Culture,* 10:1, pp.15–45.

4   Quoted in Frederic William Maitland, *The Life and Letters of Leslie Stephen* (Duckworth, London, 1906; reprinted by Thoemmes Antiquarian Books, Bristol, 1991), p.474.

5   Ibid., p.476.

6   Julia's mother, Maria Jackson, fell ill while they were living in India, and decided to return to England with her daughter. They lived at Little Holland House (destroyed in 1875, its garden making way for Melbury Road, Kensington). Maria's husband, a leading physician in Calcutta, was so dedicated to his job that he did not rejoin his wife and daughter for seven years, by which time he had retired.

7   So Virginia Woolf claims in her introductory essay on Julia Margaret Cameron in *Victorian Photographs of Famous Men and Fair Women by Julia Margaret Cameron* (Hogarth Press, London, 1926), p.xxv; reprinted in *The Essays of Virginia Woolf, Vol. 4: 1925–1928*, ed. Andrew McNeillie (Hogarth Press, London, 1994), p.377.

8   Her play, *Freshwater*, was written in 1923, revised in 1935, and published posthumously, in 2004.

9   This has now evolved into the *Oxford Dictionary of National Biography* and is available in print and online.

10 *Moments of Being* (2002), p.117.

11 Ibid.

12 Quoted in *The Life and Letters of Leslie Stephen* (1991), p.479.

13 Ibid., p.133.

14 Ibid., p.144.

15 As Julia Stephen, she later wrote the entry on Julia Margaret Cameron for *The Dictionary of National Biography*. It has now been replaced with one by Helen Barlow.

16 Quoted by John Bicknell in 'The Ramsays in Love', *Charleston Magazine,* issue 9, Spring/Summer 1994, p.8.

17 *Moments of Being* (2002), p.100.

18 Laura Stephen had such severe learning and behavioural difficulties that it was eventually decided to place her in a home where she could receive the kind of attention she evidently needed.

19 According to the *Hyde Park Gate News*, the meeting ended with Leslie Stephen thanking the Lord Mayor for permitting the meeting to take place at the Mansion House, and with the Mayor's reply that he had never before found himself at such an 'intellectual' meeting. Carlyle's house now belongs to the National Trust.

20 Quoted in *The Life and Letters of Leslie Stephen* (1991), p.300.

21 *Moments of Being* (2002), p.159.

22 Virginia Woolf, *Night and Day* (Penguin, London, 1969), pp.16–17.

23 Woolf visited Carlyle's house on four known occasions: in 1897, 1898, 1909 and 1936. In her essay 'Great Men's Houses' she describes this house, and insists 'it is no frivolous curiosity that sends us to Dickens's House and Johnson's house and Carlyle's house and Keats's house. We know them from their houses …' *The Essays of Virginia Woolf, Vol. 5: 1929–1932*, ed. Stuart N. Clarke (Chatto & Windus, London, 2009), p.294.

24 Leslie Stephen to Charles Eliot Norton, 23 October 1881, in *The Life and Letters of Leslie Stephen* (1991), p.345.

25 *Moments of Being* (2002), p.78.

26 Monk's House Papers, A5c, Special Collections, University of Sussex. Quoted in Hermione Lee, *Virginia Woolf* (Chatto & Windus, London, 1996), p.178.

27 *Moments of Being* (2002), p.123.

28 Ibid., p.47.

29 Ibid., pp.28–9.

30 An instance of this is George Duckworth's letter to Virginia Woolf, 28 May 1927: 'My dear old Goat, Just a line to say that I am in the middle of the "Lighthouse". It is a masterpiece & leaves me brimful of the music of your words. I have not dared to look to the end & am fearful that it may not end happily as I want it to do for you seem to me to be sitting at some great organ & playing a Bach fugue of your own composition …'. Special Collections, University of Sussex.

31 *Moments of Being* (2002), p.153.

32 Ibid., p.153.

33 Ibid., p.125.

34 Both versions of 'The Mausoleum Book' are in the Modern Literary Manuscripts Department of the British Museum. It was eventually published, but not in Virginia Woolf's lifetime. See Leslie Stephen, *The Mausoleum Book*, ed. Alan S. Bell (Clarendon Press, Oxford, 1977).

2 EXPERIMENTS AND REFORMS

The move out of Hyde Park Gate, Kensington, and into 46 Gordon Square, Bloomsbury, in 1904, marks a turning point in the history of the Stephen family. It signalled a search for a new identity through experiments and reforms. From now on, life was going to be different, less hidebound, more open to new things. Leslie Stephen's death had released the two sisters from a routine that had been controlled and constricted by Victorian social mores, and by their father's needs. The upheaval that autumn must have been traumatic: Hyde Park Gate was stuffed full of possessions formerly owned by Thackerays, Duckworths and Stephens: there were masses of china and glass, dozens of black tin boxes filled with letters, furniture that had been handed down,[1] as well as numerous personal mementoes. Some twenty-five years later the Stephen family's move to Gordon Square became conflated, in the mind of Vanessa Bell's son Quentin, with the arrival of Clive Bell's belongings in 1908, after his marriage to Vanessa Stephen. The drawing that Quentin produced fills an entire page in one of the *Charleston Bulletin Supplements*, which he and Virginia Woolf jointly produced in the early 1920s to amuse family and friends, usually at Christmas time.[2]

In some ways Bloomsbury and Kensington were not that different. Both were popular with professional middle-class families. Bloomsbury, however, was less fashionable than Kensington, and less populated with friends and relatives of their parents. The distance that Vanessa Stephen, the chief driver behind this move, wanted to put between herself and her siblings and their past was more psychological than geographical. And the process of liberation was helped that autumn by the Duckworth brothers' decision to separate from the Stephens and go their

'Arrival at 46 Gordon Square', from *The Messiah*, one of the *Charleston Bulletin Supplements*, c.1923. Quentin Bell's illustration of this event conflates the Stephens' arrival in 1904 with Clive Bell's arrival in 1908, creating a chaos of books, canvases and easel, guns and crates of wine, among other things.

own way. This left Vanessa free to turn her back on the darkness and claustrophobia of 22 Hyde Park Gate and paint the walls of their living rooms at Gordon Square white. She then threw Indian shawls over some of the furniture so that their colours showed up with an almost barbaric richness against the white walls. But the past was by no means wholly banished. On one side of the entrance hall she put up a row of Julia Margaret Cameron's photographs of great Victorians – Herschel, the American poet James Russell Lowell, Darwin, Leslie Stephen, Tennyson, the novelist George Meredith and Browning – opposite five of Mrs Cameron's best photographs of their mother. Vanessa remarked to her sister, of these lingering ghostly presences, that they looked very beautiful all together.

At the time of the move, Virginia was elsewhere, recuperating from a second and

Sir John Frederick Herschel photographed by Julia Margaret Cameron, 1867.

Clockwise from top left:
Robert Browning, Charles
Darwin and Thomas Carlyle
photographed by Julia
Margaret Cameron in 1865,
1868 and 1867 respectively.

Violet Dickinson at her home Burnham Wood at Welwyn in Hertfordshire, c.1904.

more severe breakdown: between April and September 1904 she had been dangerously ill and made at least one suicide attempt. Shortly after their father's death the Stephen family had taken a holiday in Pembrokeshire, then a trip to Venice with Gerald Duckworth, and had stopped in Paris for a few days before their return to London, to prepare for their imminent departure from Hyde Park Gate. However, even before they left Paris, Virginia had begun to lose her sanity.

The person, on this occasion, who played a major part in her recovery was Violet Dickinson. A woman of great character, compassion and height, she came from a family background made financially secure by generations of yeomen, merchants, bankers and squires, and lived with her brother in a house in Manchester Square, London. But her additional vantage point – the fact that she was six feet two inches tall – may account for her generous reach, her ability to look beyond the immediate, and for her independence: she had, for example, designed and built her own house, Burnham Wood, in the country at Welwyn in Hertfordshire, and transmuted part of a wood into a burgeoning garden. She had a wide circle of acquaintances and had been a close friend of Stella Duckworth. The seventeen-year difference in age between her and Virginia may at first have inhibited friendship, but in 1902, Violet had joined the Stephen family on their summer holiday at Fritham in the

New Forest, and, Virginia noted, proved to be an excellent guest – adaptable, high-spirited, warm-hearted, ready to laugh at herself and 'cleverish'.[3] Her friendship with Virginia lasted four decades, but it was at its most intense during the middle years of the first decade, and not least during Virginia's 1904 breakdown, for Violet, though untrained, had worked voluntarily in hospitals for the mentally ill.

The writer Vanessa Curtis has observed that when Virginia was brought to Violet at Welwyn, she arrived in the company of the entire Stephen–Duckworth family.[4] Three nurses were employed to help care for her, and Vanessa often went to see her. Her mind was so disturbed that, as her biographers record, she hated her nurses, distrusted Vanessa, thought the birds were singing in Greek, and was certain that Edward VII was hiding in the azalea bushes. On one occasion, she even threw herself out of a window, intent on suicide, but landed in the flower-bed unhurt.

Her mental confusion was so great that she was incapable of writing the shortest of letters. Violet Dickinson's patience and steadiness with Virginia's paranoia, violence and refusal to eat must have been severely strained. But in calmer moments the two women may have talked about writing and how to establish identity as a writer, for it was Violet who, later in the year, introduced Virginia to Margaret Lyttleton, who edited the women's pages of the weekly newspaper for the clergy, the

Violet Dickinson's home Burnham Wood, *c.*1904. Violet designed and built the house herself.

Guardian. The outcome of this was that in December 1904, by which time Virginia had most certainly recovered her wits, the newspaper published her review of a novel by the American William Dean Howells, which she had rattled off in half an hour, and followed it up with a more substantial piece, an account of her November pilgrimage to the Brontës' home at Haworth parsonage. The confident tone of both pieces promised future success, but it took another eleven years to achieve her first book. Violet, recognising the difficulties and having many contacts, may also have been the person who gave Virginia introductions to the *National Review* and the *Times Literary Supplement,* both of which became additional outlets for her early literary endeavours. Violet certainly encouraged Virginia to break into the literary world. When Virginia was well enough to join her other siblings at 46 Gordon Square, she found on her desk a gift from Violet – a china inkpot, large and deep.

Many years later, in 1936, Virginia Woolf received a letter from Violet Dickinson asking if she would like to see some letters from the past. 'Do send them,' Woolf replied, '… Letters and memoirs are my delight – how much better than novels!'[5] A large package arrived containing typed copies of the early letters Virginia had sent Violet, and which had been bound into two volumes, along with some photographs from that period and a few of Virginia's drawings. Re-reading these letters, Woolf confronted her earlier self. She wrote:

> It was extremely good of you to keep and bind up so much better than they deserved all those scattered fragments of my very disjected and egotistic youth. Do you like that girl? I'm not sure that I do, though I think she had some spirit in her, and certainly was rather ground down harshly by fate …. At points I became filled with such a gust from her tragic past, I couldn't read on. Letters seem more than anything to keep the past – out it comes, when one opens the box. And so much I'd forgotten. … But one thing emerges whole and lucid – how very good you were to me, and how very trying I was – all agog, all aquiver; and so full of storms and rhapsodies …[6]

It is a further tribute to Violet Dickinson that, before 1904 ended, this same young woman had begun giving adult-education classes in history and literature at Morley College in south London, and went on doing so for the next three years.

WRITING THE PAST

Between leaving Violet and arriving at 46 Gordon Square, Virginia had gone to Cambridge to stay with her Quaker aunt Caroline Emilia Stephen, her father's sister. She too was an early supporter of Woolf's writing. When she died in 1909, she bequeathed £2,500 to Virginia, an inheritance that brought in a modest income, almost equivalent in value to £500 in 1927, by which time Woolf was arguing that in order to write women needed £500 a year and a room of one's own. If Caroline Emilia's legacy helped make Woolf's vocation feasible, of more immediate help, in 1904, was her suggestion that her niece, while transcribing a great many of her

father's letters that autumn for his biographer Frederic Maitland, should also contribute a personal memoir. Maitland accepted this suggestion and incorporated this memoir, somewhat abruptly, into the chapter 'Sunset on the Alps' in *The Life and Letters of Leslie Stephen*. This was to be the first time that Virginia's words appeared between the covers of a book. Committing her memories to print proved restorative, and from then on writing the past was something that, in different ways, she explored in almost all her work.

G. C. Beresford Photo.

Emery Walker Ph. Sc.

Leslie Stephen
December 1902

One notable example of this is the fictional reconstruction of her father as Mr Ramsay in *To the Lighthouse*. In 1928, the year after this book was published, Woolf made the extraordinary observation in her diary that had her father gone on living, his life would have ended hers, and there would have been no writing, no books.[7] Yet he is of critical importance to her literary development. He brought to their relationship donnish habits, encouraged her reading, discussed books, opened his library to her and gave her lessons between the ages of thirteen and fifteen for two hours every day. When, at the age of twenty, she embarked on an orgy of reading, he brought further books from the London Library to satisfy her needs. All her life, when reading in preparation for an essay or review, she habitually consulted her father's essays, especially those in his three-volume *Hours in a Library*, as well as his biographies and contributions to *The Dictionary of National Biography*. He shaped her literary taste and, among many other things, taught her that 'if writing is to last it must have, for its backbone, some fierce attachment to an idea'.[8]

Either her memoir in Maitland's book or her early journalism caught the attention of Henry James. He remained a family friend, having earlier been deeply moved by Julia Stephen's death. While taking a holiday in 1907 near Rye in Sussex, Virginia had gone with her brother Adrian, as well as Vanessa, to visit Henry James at his home, Lamb House. She reported to Violet Dickinson:

> Henry James fixed me with his staring blank eye – it is like a child's marble – and said 'My dear Virginia, they tell me – they tell me – they tell me – that you – as indeed being your father's daughter nay your grandfather's grandchild – the descendant I may say of a century – of a century – of quill pens and ink – ink – ink pots, yes, yes, yes, they tell me, – ahm m m – that you, that you, that you write in short.' This went on in the public street, while we all waited, as farmers wait for a hen to lay an egg – do they? – nervous, polite, now on this foot now on that. I felt like a condemned person, who sees the knife drop and stick and drop again. Never did any woman hate 'writing' as much as I do. But when I am old and famous I shall discourse like Henry James. We had to stop periodically to let him shake himself free of a phrase … and [he] told us all the scandal of Rye. 'Mr Jones has eloped, I regret to say, to Tasmania; leaving 12 little Jones, and possible a 13th to Mrs Jones, most regrettable, most unfortunate, and yet not wholly an action to which one has no private key of one's own so to speak … '[9]

Also present on this occasion was Clive Bell. A friend of Virginia's elder brother Thoby, Bell had been one of the young men who came to the weekly At Homes[10] which, soon after they settled in, the Stephens began holding at 46 Gordon Square. Aside from the painter Duncan Grant, all had gone up to Cambridge in the wake of university reform and the religious debates that had followed the publication of Darwin's *On the Origin of Species*. These had made necessary a new spirit of enquiry, particularly in relation to debates about morals and ethics, which could no longer resort unhesitatingly to religious teaching. The questions 'How should one live?' and 'What makes for the good life?' had to be thought out afresh. Much

Leslie Stephen photogravure reproduction by Emery Walker after photograph by George Charles Beresford, December 1902.

Above: Henry James, lithograph by William Rothenstein, 1898.

Opposite: Thoby Stephen photographed by George Charles Beresford, August 1906.

of the thinking around these issues had gone on at Cambridge in the confines of a private clique – the Cambridge Conversazione Society, which was better known by the name it called its members – the Apostles. Not all those who later formed the Bloomsbury Group belonged to this society, but, nevertheless, when Thoby Stephen brought his Cambridge friends to at-homes at Gordon Square and to meet his sisters, he in effect brought the Cambridge Apostolic tradition to London, for the chief coinage within the group, from first to last, was to be talk – argument, analysis, teasing, probing wit, humour, and a rejection of any form of cant.

These at-homes were not always a success. There were awkward silences, and sometimes the arrival of new and old friends, as well as one or two elderly relatives, made for an uncomfortable mix. Although an inner core of Thoby's friends soon came to the fore, it is possible that the novelty and attraction of these gatherings might have petered out. But in 1906 Thoby Stephen died. He had gone that summer to Asia Minor (now Turkey) with his two sisters, brother and Violet Dickinson, fell ill with what was thought to be typhoid but turned out to be malaria, and shortly after his return to London, when he seemed to be getting better, lost his life. This senseless death drew his friends and family together, their bond tightened by shock, sympathy and grief.

All her life Virginia Woolf remained haunted by the memory of Thoby, and by the immense promise conveyed by his character and good looks. We can catch glimpses of him, and of what he meant to Woolf, in two of her fictional characters – Jacob in *Jacob's Room* and the charismatic Percival in *The Waves*, whose untimely death similarly unites his friends. Of the dead Percival, Woolf writes: 'He would have protected. He would have done justice. About the age of forty he would have shocked the authorities. No lullaby has ever occurred to me capable of singing him to rest.'[11]

In Thoby's absence, his friends mattered even more to the two sisters. Vanessa, having previously declined an offer of marriage from Clive Bell, now accepted his second proposal. They married on 7 February 1907, and Virginia and Adrian moved to 29 Fitzroy Square. This magnificent eighteenth-century square, part of it built by Robert Adam, was then very shabby, filled with workshops, lodging houses and offices. The two Stephen siblings, with Sophie Farrell, the cook, who had worked for the Stephen family since the 1880s,[12] were said to be the only people there who had an entire house to themselves. Their near neighbour Duncan Grant made a quick pen and ink sketch of Virginia seated in an armchair (page 65), snatching the moment, as he did a couple of years later with an oil portrait of her, most of it painted on the spot while she had a long conversation with Vanessa. Virginia's time at Fitzroy Square was not entirely happy, for she and Adrian, as she later recalled, 'drove each other into perpetual frenzies of irritation or into the depths of gloom'.[13] They still held at-homes but they were strained and often ended in failure, after which Adrian and Virginia would depart to their separate bedrooms in complete silence. It puzzled Virginia that the sessions both excited and bored her: they offered mental freedom yet at the same time were deadened by silences and a sense of things unsaid. She later observed: 'It never struck me that the abstractness, the simplicity which had been so great a relief after Hyde Park Gate were largely due to the fact that the majority of the young men who came were not attracted to women.'[14] What was missing was physical attraction, and the 'lustre and illusion'[15] that at this time she began to experience at Lady Ottoline Morrell's parties in nearby Bedford Square.

LYTTON STRACHEY AND THE 'BLOOMSBERRIES'

Virginia Stephen's interest in this society hostess, the daughter of the Duke of Portland and wife of the solicitor and politician Philip Morrell, whose incontinent love life and theatrically contrived appearance made her the subject of unending gossip, has to be balanced against her simultaneous attraction to the writer and renowned homosexual Lytton Strachey, one of the so-called 'Bloomsberries'.[16] She was amused, shocked and stimulated by the wholly unorthodox Strachey who readily discerned the absurd in most situations and, far from worshipping the great, made others giggle with his mock hysteria and pronounced hypochondria. She and

Strachey corresponded with each other, in a rather self-conscious fashion. Then suddenly, in 1909, he proposed to her and she accepted. Terrified by what he had done, he wrote to her the following day, asking to withdraw his proposal which had, he explained, been brought on by a momentary 'wobble'.[17] This astonishing episode, if anything, cleared the way for a more honest relationship that lasted until Strachey's death in 1932.

At Fitzroy Square, Woolf wrote every morning and began to put in place ambitions as a writer. In the summer of 1908 she took a holiday on her own, taking rooms first in Wells, Somerset, and then at Manorbier in Pembrokeshire, so that she could work on a novel. Her new confidant on literary matters was Clive Bell, who took over this role from Violet Dickinson. Whereas before she had flirted verbally with Violet, mostly in her letters, she now did the same with Clive, in part, perhaps, as an indirect protest to Vanessa, much of whose attention was currently vested in her new-born son, Julian. It was, however, her desire to write a novel that made Clive's advice so welcome. In August 1908 she wrote to him:

> I think a great deal of my future and [how to] settle what book I am to write – how I shall re-form the novel and capture multitudes of things at present fugitive, enclose the whole, and capture infinite strange shapes. I take a good look at woods in the sunset, and fix men who are breaking stones with an intense gaze, meaning to sever them from past and future … but tomorrow I know, I shall be sitting down to the inanimate old phrases ….[18]

There may be an element of teasing hyperbole in this passage, but, nevertheless, her dissatisfaction with the current state of the novel is revealing, as is her desire to register the 'fugitive'. It is a bold statement from an author who had yet to publish

Opposite: Lytton Strachey by Simon Bussy, 1904.

Below: Lytton Strachey and Virginia Woolf at Garsington. Photographed by Lady Ottoline Morrell, June 1923.

67

Letter from Lytton Strachey to Virginia Stephen, 17 February 1909. The letter, written after he had withdrawn his proposal, reads: I'm still rather agitated and exhausted. I try to imagine you at your Green Street dinner, between Lord Dunsany and Thomas Hardy, but it's difficult. I do hope you're cheerful! As for me, I'm all of a heap, and the future seems a blank to me. But whatever happens, as you said, the important thing is that we should like each other; and we can neither of us have any doubt that we do. I hope to see Vanessa tomorrow morning. This world is so difficult to manage. Your Lytton.

TELEPHONE:- HAMPSTEAD 1090.

67, BELSIZE PARK GARDENS,

HAMPSTEAD, N.W.

Feb. 17th 1909

I'm still rather agitated and exhausted. I try to imagine you at your Green Street dinner, between Lord Dunsany and Thomas Hardy, but it's difficult. I do hope you're cheerful! As for me, I'm all of a heap, and the future seems a blank to me. But whatever happens, as you said, the important thing is that we should like each other; and we can neither of us have any doubt that we do. I hope to see Vanessa tomorrow morning. This world is so difficult to manage. Your Lytton.

a novel. Also interesting is the spatial element in her above-stated desire to 'enclose the whole, and capture infinite strange shapes'. It reminds us that her working life ran parallel with that of a painter, her sister Vanessa, who had trained at the Royal Academy Schools, and that art, in the coming years, was to have a formative influence on Woolf's modernist fiction.

Inevitably, given the place that G.F. Watts had occupied in their family history, Vanessa and Virginia went to see his memorial exhibition at the Royal Academy in January 1905, following his death the previous summer. It was a huge show, and in among the many exhibits would have been reminders of the first Little Holland House. But Watts could no longer be described as 'England's Michelangelo'. Vanessa had already concluded that, in his pursuit of great ideals and abstract ideas, he had neglected the art of painting and used it only as a half-learned language. Virginia now also experienced great disappointment in this man whom her family had once venerated. To her friend Madge Vaughan she wrote: 'By the way, the Watts show is *atrocious*; my last illusion is gone. Nessa and I walked through the rooms almost in tears. Some of his work – indeed most of it – is quite childlike.'[19]

Whereas Watts's reputation during this decade more or less collapsed and had to wait another hundred years before it would be re-examined, the legacy of James McNeill Whistler, especially his feeling for tonal harmony, proved remarkably far-reaching. It is visible in Vanessa Bell's portrait of Saxon Sydney-Turner, the most silent member of the Bloomsbury Group, who later disappeared into the Treasury, where he pursued his gift for acrostics. Whistler's influence is also visible in Francis Dodd's etching of Virginia Stephen. She first agreed to sit for her portrait in 1907, for she had not as yet developed a dislike of being a sitter. It evidently had

Saxon Sydney-Turner at the piano by Vanessa Bell, *c.*1908.

Above, left: Virginia
Stephen by Francis Dodd,
chalk drawing, 1908.

Above, right: Virginia
Stephen by Francis Dodd,
etching, 1909.

a certain novelty at this stage, as she wrote to Violet Dickinson: 'Dodd, a little New English Club artist, half drunk, and ecstatic, wishes to paint my portrait – and I am to sit from 2 to 4.30. Alone?'[20] In fact she sat for Francis Dodd on several occasions between October 1907 and July 1908, and one of his drawings of her can be found in the National Portrait Gallery collection (above left). Less well known is the etching that Dodd made, which exists in four states, the final state dated 1909 (above right). It is not known why Dodd decided to etch rather than paint, nor how it came about that Virginia posed in a suitably Whistlerian Japanese gown. The result is charming but slightly inept, giving no indication of Dodd's later reputation as a portraitist, for during the 1914–18 war he was commissioned to draw every major and admiral in the British forces.

By 1909 Vanessa Bell had arrived at a subtle handling of tone and composition. Her *Iceland Poppies* (Charleston Trust collection), when hung at the New English Art Club, had been praised by the avant-garde artist Walter Sickert. Yet, with hindsight, this period represents the quiet before the storm, for a chance meeting at

Cambridge railway station resulted in a new member of the Bloomsbury Group. He was older and more experienced than the others, and before very long he had dragged Bloomsbury out of the confines and privacy of the drawing-room into the centre of a noisy and very public debate.

ROGER FRY'S VISION

'Roger', wrote Virginia Woolf to her sister in December 1928, 'is the only civilised man I have ever met, and I continue to think him the plume in our cap; the vindication, asseveration – and all the rest of it – If Bloomsbury had produced only Roger, it would be on a par with Athens at its prime (little though this will convey to you). We dined with him, and came away – fed to the lips, but impressed almost to tears by his charm.'[21]

The tone of this passage is light, humorous, a touch exaggerated, even self-mocking, but there is no doubting Woolf's deep responsiveness to Roger Fry. She never forgot his first appearance at 46 Gordon Square, soon after his chance meeting with Clive and Vanessa Bell at Cambridge station and a train journey back to London, during which most of the talk had been about modern French art.

> He appeared, I seem to think, in a large ulster coat, every pocket of which was stuffed with a book, a paint box or something intriguing; special tips which he had bought from a little man in a back street; he had canvases under his arms; his hair flew; his eyes glowed. He had more knowledge and experience than the rest of us put together …. We started talking about *Marie-Claire* [an autobiographical novel by Marguerite Audoux]. And at once we were all launched into a terrific argument about literature. … We had to think the whole thing over again, the old skeleton arguments of primitive Bloomsbury about art and beauty took on flesh and blood. There was always some new idea afoot …[22]

Towards the end of his life, Leslie Stephen had developed a fascination with French novels. Virginia thought this worthy of mention in the short memoir of her father, written for Frederic Maitland, perhaps because an interest in French literature was still rare in England at this date. More usual was a xenophobic distrust of all things French. Thus, when Roger Fry pulled out of his pocket a recently published French novel and engaged everyone present in a lively debate about literature, he, in effect, produced a passport into Virginia's life.

Roger Fry's arrival on to the scene coincided with his involvement with French Post-Impressionism. In 1910 and 1912 he mounted in London two famous Post-Impressionist exhibitions, which introduced Britain to modern French art, something that had been largely ignored over the previous thirty years. Shortly before the first of these exhibitions, he had published 'An Essay in Aesthetics', which later reappeared in his influential collection of essays *Vision and Design* (1920). This essay posits with great clarity the shift in focus that accompanies the move

away from the Renaissance tradition into the period that gave rise to modernism. Fry argued that imitation of natural appearances was no longer necessary in art unless the emotional idea expressed is to some extent dependent upon likeness or completeness of representation. The viewer, he insists, should disregard the idea of likeness to nature when in front of a painting and should instead question whether the 'emotional elements of design' inherent in the scene have been adequately discovered. Introducing the second and more up-to-date of his two Post-Impressionist exhibitions, he wrote in the catalogue: 'These artists do not seek to give what can, after all, be but a pale reflex of reality. They do not seek to imitate form, but to create form; not to imitate life, but to create life.'

Living a few doors away from Duncan Grant, who was frequently in and out of 29 Fitzroy Square, Virginia would have been aware of the impact these two exhibitions had on the work of various young painters. The representational skills that Grant had brought to his portrait of his cousin James Strachey, painted during the

winter of 1909–10, before he had properly come into contact with French Post-Impressionism, are impressive. The handling of tone and the careful attention to the pattern in the carpet help set the figure within an illusionistic space, but they leave the decorative arrangement of the picture surface rather weak. Once the reality of a picture was seen to reside in the actual mark-making, in the rhythmic arrangement of the parts and in the colour harmonies created, illusionism, by contrast, came to seem facile, shallow and deceitful. Post-Impressionism demanded a new way of looking and making, and also new values.

WIFE AND WRITER

By the time the Second Post-Impressionist Exhibition opened at the Grafton Galleries in London, Virginia had married Leonard Woolf. He was the son of a solicitor, but in a previous generation his family had been shopkeepers. He was, in that notorious phrase Virginia Stephen wrote after agreeing to marry him, 'a penniless Jew'. Penniless? Yes. According to a balance sheet dated 11 December 1912, in Sussex University Library, he had at that time around £600 in cash and investments. But this was not inherited wealth: most of it derived from winning £690 on the Melbourne Cup sweepstake in 1908. When he first went up to Cambridge, he would have been near penniless. And he was certainly a Jew, Virginia Woolf frankly acknowledging this 'otherness'. Yet if Leonard Woolf was socially and racially different from others in the Bloomsbury Group, why was he so readily accepted into this circle of friends? Any answer to this question must acknowledge that the 'Bloomsberries', so often dismissed as cliquish, snobbish and exclusive, were in some ways *more* inclusive than most other parts of English society at this time.

Lytton Strachey, after he had retracted his proposal to Virginia, had immediately written to Leonard Woolf, who was working for the colonial service in Ceylon at the time, arguing that Leonard should return to England. 'I think there's no doubt whatever that you ought to marry her. You *would* be great enough, and you'd have the advantage of physical desire. I was in terror lest she should kiss me.' [23] Again, it was an example of judicious teasing. Leonard had seen Virginia Stephen only twice before leaving for Ceylon. The first time was in Cambridge in Thoby Stephen's rooms. She and Vanessa were wearing white dresses, large hats and carried parasols. Their beauty literally took his breath away, but he also noticed a look in their eyes, a look that warned him to be cautious, 'which belied the demureness, a look of great intelligence, hypercritical, sarcastic, satirical'. [24] As it turned out, Leonard, although he had reached high office in the colonial service and had developed rigorous administrative habits and a sharp attention to detail, did return to England and did propose; and Virginia accepted. Together they sent a sheet of notepaper to Lytton on which was written, 'Ha, Ha! Virginia Stephen, Leonard Woolf' (page 77), from which Lytton could deduce that his wish had been fulfilled. They were married in St Pancras Town Hall.

Virginia Stephen now mutates into Virginia Woolf, her identity altering with this change of status and name. The question 'Who am I?' must have crossed her mind before and after the date of her wedding, and would have been exacerbated by the fact that in 1911–12 she sat on four occasions for portraits by Vanessa Bell. None is dated, but stylistically they all belong to the pre-1914 period. In one instance Roger Fry was also present, and Woolf posed for both artists with her lower arms crossed on the table in front of her. These two portraits reflect differing competencies on the part of each artist, as well as different intersubjective relations between artist and sitter (pages 78–9). Awareness of how differently Woolf's identity is

Above: Virginia Woolf in an
armchair by Vanessa Bell,
*c.*1912.

Opposite: Virginia Woolf by
Vanessa Bell, *c.*1912.

constructed in both portraits may have encouraged Bell to experiment further, for in the other three portraits of Woolf, painted at this time, she blurs, veils and finally entirely removes the facial features.

Virginia Woolf in a deckchair by Vanessa Bell, c.1912.

When we look at a portrait, our attention roves around the picture, sometimes finding details that relate to the character, profession or social status of the sitter. In any portrait our interest usually climaxes when we reach the face, even if we do not share the old belief that the face offers an index to a sitter's moral character. It is tempting to see in Vanessa Bell's four portraits of Virginia from this period a deliberate progression towards complete abstraction. This progression may be a fallacy, however, for, as mentioned, the paintings are not dated, and the one now in the Smith College Museum, Massachusetts (page 81), in which the face is obliterated by a series of marks veiling the face, may precede the one mentioned above, which now belongs to the National Trust (page 79).[25] But even if Bell did not follow a logical progression, these portraits, taken as a group, demonstrate a move from representation to abstraction. The facial features are correctly positioned in the National Trust portrait, deliberately blurred in the National Portrait Gallery likeness, where the sitter is shown crocheting (page 80), emphatically veiled at Smith College Museum, while in the small portrait of Woolf in a deckchair, the face is suggested by a blank space (opposite). This negative area interrupts the narrative of the portrait and obliges the viewer to activate it with thought, memories or metonymic associations. With hindsight, it can also be argued that this seemingly blank space becomes an eloquent expression of the interiority that Woolf was to search for in her novels. It also suggests that something has been withheld, remains unknowable. It brings to mind the essay 'On Being Ill', which Woolf wrote many years later. 'We do not know our own souls,' she writes, 'let alone the souls of others.'[26] The absent face acts like a pregnant silence, a quality that Woolf admired in some of her friends. In her first novel, *The Voyage Out*, she makes the would-be novelist Terence Hewet say: 'I would like to write about Silence; the things people don't say …'

A SEVERE DEPRESSION

It is probable that some, if not all, of these portraits of Woolf were painted at Asheham, a small Regency house that sat in an isolated position several miles from Lewes in Sussex. For some years this remained a country retreat, shared by the two sisters and visited by their friends. It seemed to encourage experimentation, as on the occasion when Lytton Strachey sat outside near a garden wall and was painted by Fry, Grant and Vanessa Bell in colours that owed more to the French artist Paul Gauguin than to the Sussex landscape. It was here, as well as in London, that Woolf wrote *The Voyage Out*, the manuscript remaining for some years forgotten in this house after the book was published. Meanwhile, Leonard, though making a living through journalism, also wrote his first novel, *The Village in the Jungle* (1913), based on his experiences in Ceylon. He dedicated it to 'V.W.' in a touchingly awkward verse:

Conversation at Asheham House by Vanessa Bell, 1912. Conversation was an essential medium for Bloomsbury.

Asheham House, Sussex, c.1911. This small Gothic Revival house was a country retreat initially shared by the two sisters, and remained a bolt-hole for Leonard and Virginia Woolf up until 1919.

I've given you all the little, that I've to give;
You've given me all, that for me is all there is;
So now I just give back to you what you have given –
If there is anything to give in this.

In among the 'all' that she had given him was fairly constant anxiety over her state of mind and health. In 1913 he knew that a further bout of mental instability lay ahead when her headaches and insomnia returned, and she began to refuse to eat. For the next three years she was intermittently ill. There had been a bad period in the summer of 1910, when Virginia had been sent for six weeks to a private nursing home in Twickenham, Surrey, that specialised in patients with nervous disorders. She had hated it, but, despite this, she was sent there again in 1913, only to endure a severe depression. She emerged suicidal and was taken to see two new specialists, both of whom recommended she be returned to a sanatorium. Before this happened she took an overdose of the barbiturate veronal and had to have her stomach pumped to save her life. Her recuperation took place at George Duckworth's house near East Grinstead in Sussex.

When the First World War began in September 1914, the tremor in one of Leonard's hands, as well as his wife's illness, spared him from having to decide whether or not he was a conscientious objector. He had already associated himself with Fabianism and the Women's Co-operative Guild, and had written on consumer co-operative socialism. During the war, his critique of imperialism and capitalism coalesced, and he wrote two Fabian reports on the need for international government, which are said to have formed the basis of the League of Nations and subsequently the United Nations. All the while, in another part of his mind he was coping with his wife's mental collapse, for in February 1915 she underwent her most severe attack of ill health, became incoherent and at one point fell into a coma. They had already moved out of central London, to Richmond, in order to give her peace and quiet. They stayed in temporary accommodation at 17 The Green while waiting to take over Hogarth House, which occupied half of a Georgian brick building. But on 25 March 1915 Leonard moved in alone, as Virginia was in a nursing home. The next day *The Voyage Out* was published. Its author scarcely registered the event and was too ill to read the reviews. When she finally moved into Hogarth House, there were four nurses on hand to care for her around the clock, an expense that was more than Leonard could afford. In April he wrote to Violet Dickinson:

Dear Violet,
I had meant to let you know how things went. I'm afraid they are very bad. She is worse than I have ever seen her before. She hasn't had a moment's sleep in the last 60 hours. I have seen Craig again this afternoon. He is very pessimistic. And yet a fortnight ago she seemed to be doing so splendidly. She ate so well and put on weight, & even now she is a stone heavier than she was ever in her life before. I would let you know if there was anything you could do but I'm afraid there is nothing that anyone can do.
Yours,
Leonard[27]

Lucidity and more rational behaviour eventually replaced violence and screaming, but it distressed Vanessa to find that her sister's personality had changed. 'She won't see Leonard at all & has taken against all men. She says the most malicious & cutting things she can think of to everyone & they are so clever they always hurt. But what was the worst thing to me was a small book of new poems by Frances Cornford [*Spring Morning* (1915)], which has just come out which Virginia has annotated with what are meant to be stinging sarcasms and illustrations. They are simply like rather nasty schoolboy wit and not even amusing.'[28] Both the poems and the wood engravings by another Darwin, Gwen Raverat, had irritated her, and on a double-page spread on which was printed 'To a Fat Lady Seen from a Train' and 'A Wasted Day', Woolf has scribbled: 'Darwins ought not to be allowed to paint or write but only to sit in the fields naked.' Nearby is an angry pastel drawing of a woman.

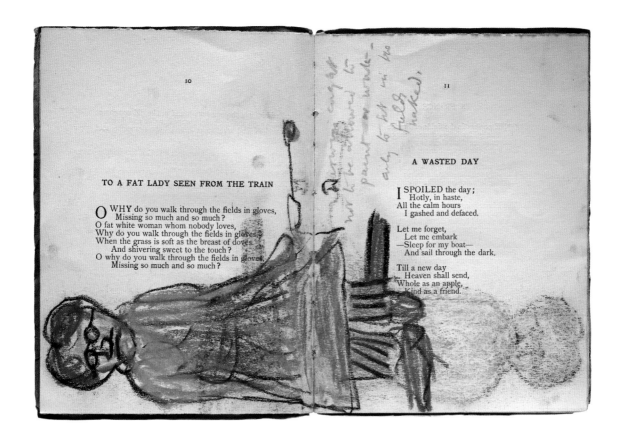

TO A FAT LADY SEEN FROM THE TRAIN

O WHY do you walk through the fields in gloves,
    Missing so much and so much?
O fat white woman whom nobody loves,
Why do you walk through the fields in gloves,
When the grass is soft as the breast of doves
    And shivering sweet to the touch?
O why do you walk through the fields in gloves,
    Missing so much and so much?

A WASTED DAY

I SPOILED the day;
    Hotly, in haste,
All the calm hours
    I gashed and defaced.

Let me forget,
    Let me embark
—Sleep for my boat—
    And sail through the dark.

Till a new day
    Heaven shall send,
Whole as an apple,
    Kind as a friend.

The words and drawings that Virginia Woolf has scribbled onto this double-page spread from *Spring Morning* (1915), a book of poems by Frances Cornford, illustrated elsewhere by Gwen Raverat's woodcuts, gives a vivid insight into her mental illness at this time. Cornford and Raverat were the grandchildren of Charles Darwin.

It took months for her mind to recover and for her former self to return. By November 1915 she was able to manage without a nurse and gradually returned to normal life. Leonard Woolf knew they needed to proceed cautiously. Yet before long their joint talents found a fresh outlet, and Hogarth House lent its name to a surprising new adventure.

NOTES

1. Certain items of furniture travelled on and can be found at Charleston, the Bloomsbury house at Firle, near Lewes, East Sussex, which is now open to the public for seven months of the year.

2. These have now been published in one volume by the British Library, in facsimile, but not, however, in the same size as the originals.

3. Virginia Woolf's full description of Violet Dickinson at this time is quoted in Vanessa Curtis, *Virginia Woolf's Women* (Sutton Publishing, Stroud, 2003), p.72.

4. Ibid., p.75.

5. *Leave the Letters Till We're Dead: The Letters of Virginia Woolf, Vol. 6: 1936–1941*, ed. Nigel Nicolson, assisted by Joanne Trautmann (Hogarth Press, London, 1980), p.87.

6. Ibid., p.90.

7. 'His life would have entirely ended mine. What would have happened? No writing, no books; – inconceivable.' *The Diary of Virginia Woolf: Vol. 3: 1929–1930*, ed. Anne Olivier Bell (Hogarth Press, London, 1980), p.208.

8. Lyndall Gordon on Virginia Woolf in *The Oxford Dictionary of National Biography* (online).

9. *The Flight of the Mind: The Letters of Virginia Woolf, Vol. 1: 1888–1912*, ed. Nigel Nicolson, assisted by Joanne Trautmann (Hogarth Press, London, 1975), p.306.

10. 'At Home' was the familiar phrase used on invitation cards, announcing the time, date and address at which an informal gathering or party was to be held at a person's house.

11. Virginia Woolf, *The Waves* (1931), ed. Gillian Beer (Oxford University Press, Oxford, 2008), p.203.

12. Details about Sophie Farrell's life are provided by Alison Light in *Mrs Woolf and Her Servants: the Hidden Heart of Domestic Service*, (Fig Tree, London, 2007). Woolf's complex relationship with her servants is summed up in her diary entry for 16 June 1930: 'Oh to be rid of servants – for all the emotions they breed – trust, suspicion, benevolence, gratitude, philanthropy,

are necessarily bad.' *The Diary of Virginia Woolf, Vol. 3 1938–1930*, p.305.

13. Virginia Woolf, *Moments of Being* (2002), ed. Hermione Lee (Pimlico, London, 2002), p.54.

14. Ibid.

15. Ibid., p.55.

16. Molly MacCarthy, wife of Desmond MacCarthy, both of whom were part of the group, is said to have coined this nickname.

17. To Leonard Woolf, Strachey admitted: 'I was brought to it by the horror of my present wobble and the imagination of the paradise of married peace.' From *The Letters of Lytton Strachey*, eds Paul Levy and Penelope Marcus (Penguin Books, London, 2006), p.174.

18. *The Letters of Virginia Woolf, Vol. I*, p.356.

19. Ibid., p.174.

20. Ibid., p.297.

21. *A Change of Perspective: The Letters of Virginia Woolf: Vol. 3: 1923–1928*, ed. Nigel Nicolson, assisted by Joanne Trautmann (Hogarth Press, London, 1977), p.566.

22. *Moments of Being* (2002), p.57.

23. *The Letters of Lytton Strachey* (2006), p.173.

24. Leonard Woolf, *Sowing: An Autobiography of the Years 1880 to 1904* (Hogarth Press, London, 1960), p.184.

25. The reason for this remark is that the portrait now belonging to Smith College Museum is stylistically similar to a small portrait by Bell of Lytton Strachey (Private Collection, USA). This too is undated, but both portraits appear to belong with Bell's very early experiments with a Post-Impressionist style in and around 1911.

26. In *The Essays of Virginia Woolf: Vol. 4: 1925–1928*, ed. Andrew McNeillie (Hogarth Press, London, 1994), p.320.

27. 28 April 1915, Berg Collection, New York Public Library.

28. Vanessa Bell to Roger Fry, 25 June 1915, quoted in Quentin Bell, *Virginia Woolf: A Biography, Vol. 2: Mrs Woolf 1912–1941* (Chatto & Windus, London, 1972), p.26.

3 'PAINTING AND WRITING HAVE MUCH TO TELL EACH OTHER …'

Hogarth House and Richmond did indeed prove therapeutic. Woolf still had relative ease of access to central London, thanks to the London Underground's District Line, but she resented being kept at arm's length from its social and literary world. Yet at Richmond she recovered her mental powers and embarked on a fertile period of innovation; here, and at Asheham, which remained their country retreat, she began to shape the modern novel. The construction of her identity expands further through her role as publisher, with the onset of the Hogarth Press. Running parallel with this venture, and alongside her thinking about fiction, is her growing awareness that certain pictures – those by Paul Cézanne, for example – had a capacity to 'press on some nerve, to stimulate, to excite'.[1]

A moment of this kind may have occurred in July 1916. She and Leonard spent a long weekend at Wissett in Suffolk, where Vanessa had set up home in a rented farmhouse with Duncan Grant and David Garnett so that both men could undertake farmwork while seeking exemption from military service as conscientious objectors. Here Vanessa repainted *The Conversation* (overleaf), or *Three Women*, as it was then called, and which had begun life in 1913. By 1916, the Post-Impressionist interest in bold colour had been dimmed by war. The repainting introduced a greater sobriety in the colouring in the women's clothes, which seems slightly at odds with the expressive freedom in the handling of representation. There is something intentionally humorous about the way the two women on the right bend forward, intent on hearing what is being explained to them by the third woman, who uses a hand gesture to underline her speech. Behind, between curtains as simplified and sculptural as the motifs in Pablo Picasso's so-called 'negroid' period,

The Matisse Room at the Second Post-Impressionist Exhibition by Roger Fry, 1912 (detail, page 107).

The Conversation by
Vanessa Bell, 1913–16.

are some flowers, white, yellow and orange-red, set against the green lawn beyond. This sudden burst of strong colour hints at another level of signification. The colours relate to the flowers, but also, like speech bubbles, they evoke the babble of conversation, the narrative of which, however, is denied to the spectator. An echo of this picture can be found in Woolf's final novel *Between the Acts* (1941), where she describes nursemaids rolling words 'like sweets on their tongues, which, as they thinned to transparency, gave off pink, green and sweetness'.[2]

Woolf appears not to have seen *The Conversation* again for some years, until it was included in an exhibition in 1928. This painting and another by Grant caused her to write: 'I had forgotten the extreme brilliancy and flow and wit and ardour of these works.' Her letter to her sister continues: 'But I maintain that you are into the bargain a satirist, a conveyor of impressions about human life, a short story writer of great wit, & able to bring off a situation in a way that arouses my envy. I wonder if I could write *Three Women* in prose?'[3]

This suggestion was never fulfilled, but evidently the painting, in 1916, had made an impact. The following year Woolf wrote 'The Mark on the Wall'. It is also a spirited, teasing performance. But in order to publish such an experimental piece, she needed an outlet untrammelled by the conventions of the day.

Leonard and Virginia had earlier considered learning the art of printing. What catapulted them into action was the arbitrary sighting of a small hand-press in the shop window of the Excelsior Printing and Supply Company, as they walked down Farringdon Street, near Holborn. Leonard went inside to enquire its price. For £19 5s 6d he bought this press, together with some type and a small instruction booklet. Four months later, in July 1917, he and Virginia produced their first publication under the imprint of the Hogarth Press. Called *Two Stories*, it contained Virginia's 'The Mark on the Wall' and Leonard's 'Three Jews'. It took them two months to create this thirty-four page booklet, partly because they worked only part time on the press, but also because they did not have enough type to produce more than two pages at a time. Owing to the tremor in Leonard's hand, which left him unable to handle type, there had to be a clear division of labour. It was Virginia who broke up the great blocks of type and arranged the letters and fonts in their correct partitions, sometimes muddling her n's and h's. It was she who filled the composing stick, which held four or five lines of type. Once these had been transferred to the galley, she began again, until she had set enough lines to fill a page. 'We get so absorbed,' she wrote to Vanessa Bell, 'we can't stop; I see that real printing will devour one's entire life. I am going to see Katherine Mansfield, to get a story from her; please experiment with [the colouring of] papers [for covers] …'[4]

Once the type pages had been locked into position, Leonard attended to the inking process, inserted the paper into the press, checked its register and, after the

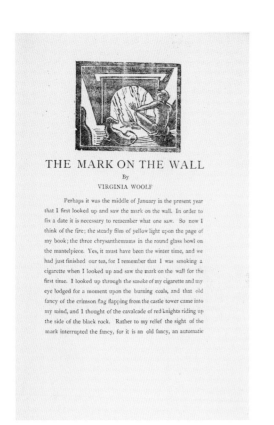

THE MARK ON THE WALL
By
VIRGINIA WOOLF

Perhaps it was the middle of January in the present year that I first looked up and saw the mark on the wall. In order to fix a date it is necessary to remember what one saw. So now I think of the fire; the steady film of yellow light upon the page of my book; the three chrysanthemums in the round glass bowl on the mantelpiece. Yes, it must have been the winter time, and we had just finished our tea, for I remember that I was smoking a cigarette when I looked up and saw the mark on the wall for the first time. I looked up through the smoke of my cigarette and my eye lodged for a moment upon the burning coals, and that old fancy of the crimson flag flapping from the castle tower came into my mind, and I thought of the cavalcade of red knights riding up the side of the black rock. Rather to my relief the sight of the mark interrupted the fancy, for it is an old fancy, an automatic

PRELUDE

KATHERINE MANSFIELD

Above, left: The Hogarth Press's first publication *Two Stories*, which includes Virginia's 'The Mark on the Wall' and Leonard's 'Three Jews', 1917.

Above, right: *Prelude* by Katherine Mansfield, Hogarth Press, July 1917. The motif on the cover was designed by John Duncan Fergusson, but disliked by the Woolfs and only used on a small number of the 300 copies printed.

first printing, would turn the paper over so that it could be printed on the other side.[5] In this homespun fashion, they had, by May 1919, added four items to their published list, in editions of no more than 300 copies, which were sold by subscription. These were Katherine Mansfield's *Prelude* (which, at sixty-eight pages, took almost nine months to produce); *Kew Gardens* by Virginia Woolf; *Poems* by T.S. Eliot; and J. Middleton Murry's *Critic in Judgement*. Leonard rated the publication of Eliot's *Poems* a red-letter day for the press, for it included 'Sweeney among the Nightingales', 'Mr. Eliot's Sunday Morning Service' and 'Whispers of Immortality'. He also recollected that they spent much time finding 'beautiful, uncommon, and sometimes cheerful paper for binding our books', including some brilliantly patterned papers from Czechoslovakia, Japanese papers, and marbled papers, made for the Hogarth Press by Roger Fry's daughter Pamela.[6]

When the hand-press broke down or the demand for publications required speedier production, the Woolfs made use of a machine owned by a local printer. Both husband and wife were offhand about their new venture, Leonard claiming that he had hoped the business of printing would act as therapy for Virginia, while she, in turn, saw the press as a means of deflecting the hold that Beatrice and Sydney Webb's Fabian socialism had on Leonard. But, in fact, by 1923 they had published two modernist masterpieces: Hope Mirrlees' *Paris: A Poem* (1920),[7] a 650-line

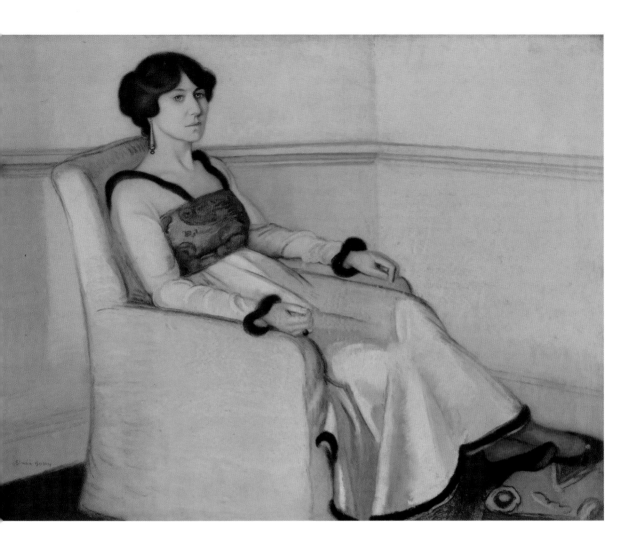

Hope Mirrlees by Simon Bussy, *c.*1919.

stream-of-consciousness poem about post-war Paris, beginning with advertising slogans and phrases picked up on the Métro, and T.S. Eliot's *The Waste Land* (1923, overleaf). The first, with its print-run of only 175 copies, was quickly forgotten after its publication, and Mirrlees herself, after her conversion to Catholicism, refused to permit its inclusion in an anthology,[8] and, in her own annotated copy, cancelled out passages that she had come to regard as blasphemous. Not until after her death was the poem republished (in 2007), with accompanying notes by Julia Briggs, which helped to attract scholarly attention and a new generation of readers. The second publication, on the other hand, for which about 460 copies were printed, immediately became a foundational modernist text. Both were typeset by Virginia Woolf, *Paris* proving the more difficult owing to its idiosyncratic typographical effects (pages 98–9).

They had drifted into publishing, Leonard Woolf admitted, with the notion of producing things that more commercial publishers would not take. Gerald

Duckworth's publishing house had accepted Virginia's *The Voyage Out*, effectively a *bildungsroman*, in which the young Rachel Vinrace journeys to South America and towards greater self-knowledge. Her second novel was also committed to Duckworth's, but her excitement over the Hogarth Press, and the freedom it gave to publish what they wished, hints at the resentment she now felt at having to subject her work to the editorial constraints of her half-brother's firm. Although *The Voyage Out* in places scintillates in its use of dialogue and description, evidence has been found among its drafts that Woolf toned down passages on homosexuality, colonialism and the Suffrage movement.[9] The conservative nature of Duckworth's makes it unlikely they would have been interested in *Two Stories,* with its rather folksy illustrations and cover design by the artist Dora Carrington, and, inside, the untethered, brilliantly imaginative short story 'The Mark on the Wall'.

It opens with the word 'Perhaps' and proceeds to unfold the instability in things. Initially, the narrator's attention darts around the room in memory, trying to identify the precise month in which the mark had first been noticed, before reflecting on 'how readily our thoughts swarm upon a new object'. This was Woolf's first attempt to relate a tale, not in terms of character, plot and external appearances, but to catch the flight of the mind, stimulated, in this instance, by an arbitrary detail. The piece was startlingly fresh and new. As it unfurls, the narrator ponders, with almost dizzying speed, the mystery of life, the inaccuracy of thought, and how easily things are lost:

Paris by Hope Mirrlees, Hogarth Press, 1920. Right: Patterned paper cover made by the Woolfs, with pasted-on label. Opposite: Pages showing the idiosyncratic typographical effects required by the poem, most of which Virginia Woolf set. Mirrlees's strike-throughs delete the passages she felt to be blasphemous after her conversion to Catholicism.

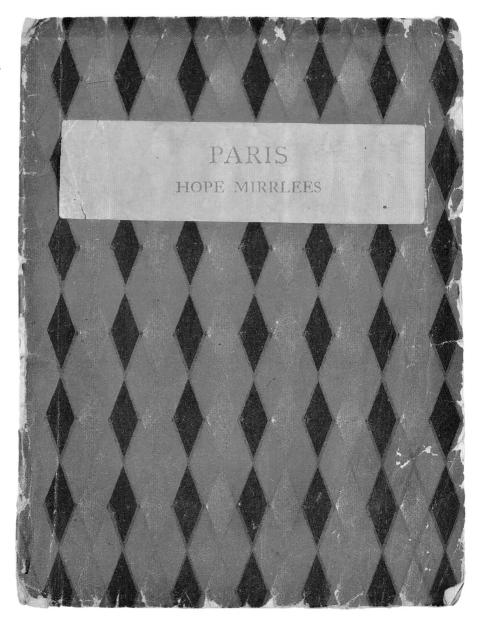

All the time
Scentless Lyons' roses,
Icy,
Plastic,
Named after wives of Mayors. . . .

Did Ingres paint a portrait of Madame Jacquemart
André?

In the Louvre
The Pietà of Avignon,
L'Olympe,
Giles,
Mantegna's Seven Deadly Sins,
The Chardins ;

They arise, serene and unetiolated, one by one from
their subterranean sleep of five long years.

Like Duncan they slept well.

President Wilson grins like a dog and runs about the
city, sniffing with innocent enjoyment the diluvial
urine of Gargantua.

The poplar buds are golden chrysalids ;
The Ballet of green Butterflies
Will soon begin.

(8)

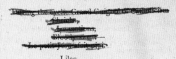

Lilac

SPRING IS SOLOMON'S LITTLE SISTER; SHE HAS NO
BREASTS.

LAIT SUPERIEUR
DE LA
FERME DE RAMBOUILLET

ICI ON CONSULTE
LE BOTTIN

CHARCUTERIE
COMESTIBLES DE 1re CHOIX

APERITIFS

ALIMENTS DIABETIQUES
DEUIL EN 24 HEURES

Messieursetdames

Little temples of Mercury ;
The circumference of their *templum*
A nice sense of scale,

(9)

Cloacæ
Hot india-rubber
Poudre de riz
Algerian tobacco
Monsieur Jourdain in the blue and red of the Zouaves
Is premier danseur in the Ballet Turque
'Ya bon !
Mamamouchi

YANKEES--"and say besides that in Aleppo once..."
Many a *Mardi Gras* and *Carême Prenant* of the
Peace Carnival ;

Crape veils,
Mouths pursed up with lip-salve as if they had just said :
Cho - co - lat . . .
"Elles se balancent sur les hanches."

Lizard-eyes,
Assyrian beards,
Boots with cloth tops—

The tart little race, whose brain, the Arabs said, was
one of the three perches of the Spirit of God.

Ouiouioui, c'est passionnant—on en a pour son argent.
Le fromage n'est pas un plat logique.

A a a a a oui c'est un délicieux garçon
Il me semble que toute femme sincère doit se retrouver
en Anna Karénine.

(12)

Never the catalepsy of the Teuton
What time
Subaqueous
Cell on cell
Experience
Very slowly
Is forming up
Into something beautiful—awful—huge

The coming to . . . . . .
Thick halting speech—the curse of vastness.

The first of May

T
h
e
r
e
i
s
n
o
l
i
l
y
o
f

(13)

The wonder is that I've any clothes on my back, that I sit surrounded by solid furniture at this moment. Why, if one wants to compare life to anything, one must liken it to being blown through the Tube at fifty miles an hour – landing at the other end without a single hairpin in one's hair! Shot out at the feet of God entirely naked! Tumbling head over heels in the asphodel meadows like brown paper parcels pitched down a shoot [*sic*] in the post office! With one's hair flying back like the tail of a race-horse. Yes, that seems to express the rapidity of life, the perpetual waste and repair; all so casual, all so haphazard …

Some years later Woolf recollected in a letter to Ethel Smyth the exhilaration she had felt when writing this short story. She was, at this time, working on her second novel, *Night and Day* (1919), and pursuing a narrative that followed the conventions of Victorian or Edwardian fiction; but at other moments she let off steam by writing experimental short stories. 'I shall never forget the day I wrote 'The Mark on the Wall' – all in a flash, as if flying, after being kept stone-breaking for months…. How I trembled with excitement; and then Leonard came in, and I drank my milk, and concealed my excitement, and wrote, I suppose, another page of that interminable *Night and Day*.'[10]

It must have been the roving consciousness in 'The Mark on the Wall' that brought Harriet Shaw Weaver, editor of the literary magazine *The Egoist*, to Richmond in order to deliver into the hands of the Woolfs the first four chapters of James Joyce's *Ulysses*, with the request that they print them. Virginia read these and found the scatological material irritating, but nevertheless recognised the importance of what Joyce was doing. To Harriet Shaw Weaver, she wrote:

> We have read the chapters of Mr Joyce's novel with great interest, and we wish that we could offer to print it. But the length is an insuperable difficulty to us at present. We can get no one to help us, and at our rate of progress a book of 300 pages would take at least two years to produce – which is, of course, out of the question for you or Mr Joyce. We very much regret this as it is our aim to produce writing of merit which the ordinary publisher refuses. Our equipment is so small however, that we are finding it difficult to bring out a book of [more] than 100 pages. We have tried to buy a larger press but without success, and therefore we are afraid that it is useless to attempt anything more ambitious.[11]

Another factor behind this decision may have been the claim of two leading printers, to whom Leonard showed the manuscript, that, owing to the obscenities, publication would lead to prosecution.

Virginia Woolf was impressed but also disturbed by Joyce's chapters. A strong antipathy – 'Leonard is already 30 pages deep. I look, and sip, and shudder' – is one of her earliest recorded reactions. Elsewhere, in her reading notes, she admitted to being 'bewildered and befogged'.[12] But she was deeply intrigued to discover that Joyce's pursuit of consciousness ran parallel with her own. She puzzled over him for many years, at one moment famously comparing the writing of *Ulysses*

T.S. Eliot and Virginia Woolf in the Green Room, Garsington. Photographed by Lady Ottoline Morrell, June 1924.

to the 'scratching of pimples on the body of the bootboy at Claridges' (a remark sent to Lytton Strachey),[13] at others, arriving at more balanced views. A hint of her perplexity in relation to Joyce is caught in the summary she wrote after his death:

> Then Joyce is dead – Joyce about a fortnight younger than I am. I remember Miss Weaver, in wool gloves, bringing Ulysses in typescript to our tea table at Hogarth House. Roger I think sent her. Would we devote our lives to printing it? The indecent pages looked so incongruous: she was spinsterly, buttoned up. And the pages reeked with

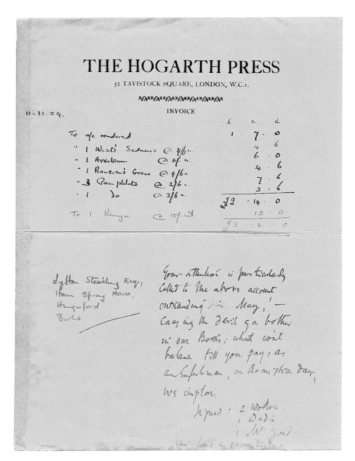

Hogarth Press bill addressed to Lytton Strachey, 11 November 1924. Message in Virginia Woolf's hand: Your attention is particularly called to the above account outstanding since May! – Causing the devil of a bother in our books; which won't balance till you pay; as an Englishman, on Armistice Day, we implore. Signed: 2 Woolves, 1 Dadie, 1 Mrs Joad. In love & reverence

indecency. I put it in the drawer of the inlaid cabinet. One day Katherine Mansfield came, & I had it out. She began to read, ridiculing: then suddenly said, But there's something in this: a scene that should figure I suppose in the history of literature. He was about the place, but I never saw him. Then I remember Tom [Eliot] in Ottoline's room at Garsington saying – it was published then – how could anyone write again after achieving the immense prodigy of the last chapter? He was for the first time in my knowledge, rapt, enthusiastic. I bought the blue paper book, & read it here one summer I think with spasms of wonder, of discovery, & then again with long lapses of intense boredom.[14]

At the time of her first encounter with *Ulysses*, Woolf still had her feet in two camps: she was writing *Night and Day,* using a traditional narrative for an allegory based on the Stephen family's struggle for freedom, and at the same she was experimenting with short stories. One of these, *Kew Gardens,* as mentioned, was published by the Hogarth Press in 1919, as a stand-alone title, with two woodcut illustrations by Vanessa Bell. This relatively primitive print medium, which requires economy of statement, well suited the haphazard flow of men and women who straggle through the gardens, amid plants, flowers, dragonflies and the zigzag of butterflies (pages

104–105). The harmonious relationship between image and text in *Kew Gardens* points again to Woolf's interest in the dialogue between art and literature. Earlier, in November 1917, Roger Fry had asked her, while she dined with him and Clive Bell, whether she founded her writing on texture or structure. The question, which derived from Fry's familiarity with the visual arts, reverberated in her mind, and became part of her thinking about the aesthetic of the novel. 'I connected structure with plot,' she noted at the time, 'and therefore said texture.'[15] This same year she expressed dissatisfaction with the current state of fiction in her review of Arnold Bennett's *Books and Persons* in the *Times Literary Supplement*. She objects to his 'infantile realism' and his concern with inessentials, and wonders what will happen to the novel if writers do with words what the Post-Impressionists did with paint.

It was Fry who drew forth her most salient remark about Joyce, at the time when she first read him: 'It's an interesting experiment; he leaves out the narrative and tries to give the thoughts …'[16] She was to extrapolate on this idea in 'Modern Novels' (1919), an essay for the *Times Literary Supplement*, where she strikes out against certain male novelists of the previous generation – H.G. Wells, Arnold Bennett and John Galsworthy. Aspects of this essay were developed in 'Mr Bennett and Mrs Brown' (1923), after which 'Modern Novels' was revised, becoming 'Modern Fiction', as found in her first collection of essays, *The Common Reader* (1925). In preparation for its first appearance, as 'Modern Novels', she had read eight chapters of *Ulysses*, and in the article cites Joyce as a novelist striking out for freedom and fresh air after the stuffy materialism of the Edwardian novel. The example of *Ulysses*, which follows the movements and thoughts of two characters in the course of one day, provoked her directive: 'Examine for a moment an ordinary mind on an ordinary day. The mind receives a myriad of impressions – trivial, fantastic, evanescent, or engraved with the sharpness of steel. From all sides they come, an incessant shower of innumerable atoms; and as they fall, as they shape themselves into the life of Monday or Tuesday, the accent falls differently from of old; the moment of importance came not here but there.' This quotation, taken from the later version of this essay, introduced the phrase 'Monday or Tuesday', which Woolf had used in 1921, for her first published collection of short stories. 'Life is not a serie of gig lamps, symmetrically arranged,' her essay continues; 'life is a luminous halo, a semi-transparent envelope surrounding us from the beginning of consciousness to the end. Is it not the task of the novelist to convey this unknown and uncircumscribed spirit, whatever aberration or complexity it may display…?'[17] It is hardly surprising that she went and bought her own copy of Ulysses in 1922, ten weeks after it was published.

Again, her reactions were mixed. 'I finished Ulysses, & think it is a mis-fire,' she wrote in her diary. 'Genius it has I think; but of the inferior water. The book is diffuse. It is brackish. It is pretentious. It is underbred, not only in the obvious sense, but in the literary sense.'[18] Yet however conflicted her response, she paid unqualified tribute to its author when asked by a desiccated cabinet minister at a luncheon party, 'Who are our promising litterateurs?' Unhesitatingly, she replied, 'Joyce'.[19]

Kew Gardens by
Virginia Woolf, Hogarth
Press, 1919. Marbled paper
cover with pasted-on label.
Two woodcut illustrations
by Vanessa Bell show a
caterpillar and a butterfly
(right), and two women
walking through the
gardens (opposite).

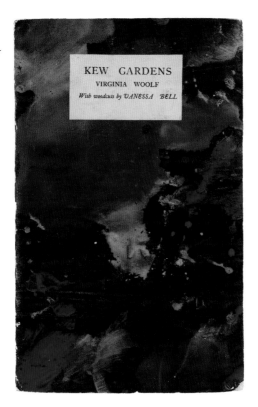

KEW GARDENS
VIRGINIA WOOLF
With woodcuts by VANESSA BELL

wavering from them as if they were flames lolling from the thick waxen bodies of candles. Voices. Yes, voices. Wordless voices, breaking the silence suddenly with such depth of contentment, such passion of desire, or, in the voices of children, such freshness of surprise; breaking the silence? But there was no silence; all the time the motor omnibuses were turning their wheels and changing their gear; like a vast nest of Chinese boxes all of wrought steel turning ceaselessly one within another the city murmured; on the top of which the voices cried aloud, and the petals of myriads of flowers flashed their colours into the air.

Printed by L. and V. Woolf at The Hogarth Press, Richmond

by William upon whose face the look of stoical patience grew slowly deeper and deeper.

Following his steps so closely as to be slightly puzzled by his gestures, came two elderly women of the lower middle class, one stout and ponderous, the other rosy cheeked and nimble. Like most people of their station they were frankly fascinated by any signs of eccentricity betokening a disordered brain especially in the well-to-do; but they were too far off to be certain whether the gestures were merely eccentric or genuinely mad. After they had scrutinised the old man's back in silence for a moment and given each other a queer sly look, they went on energetically piecing together their very complicated dialogue:

"Nell, Bert, Lot, Cess, Phil, Pa, he says, I says, she says, I says, I says, I says—"

"My Bert, Sis, Bill, Grandad, the old man, sugar,
    Sugar, flour kippers greens,
    Sugar, sugar, sugar."

The ponderous woman looked through the pattern of falling words at the flowers standing cool, firm, and upright in the earth, with a curious expression. She saw them as a sleeper waking from a heavy sleep sees a brass candlestick reflecting the light in an unfamiliar way, and closes his eyes and opens them, and, seeing the brass candlestick again, finally starts broad awake and stares at the candlestick with all his powers. So the heavy woman came to a standstill opposite the oval shaped flower bed, and ceased even to pretend to listen to what the other woman was saying. She stood there, letting the words fall over her, swaying the top part of her body slowly backwards and forwards, looking at the flowers. Then she suggested that they should find a seat and have their tea.

The snail had now considered every possible method of reaching his goal without going round the dead leaf or climbing over it. Let alone the effort needed for climbing a leaf, he was doubtful whether the thin texture which vibrated with such an alarming crackle when touched even by the tip of his horns would bear his weight; and this determined him finally to creep beneath it, for there was a point where the leaf curved high enough from the ground to admit him. He had just inserted his head in the opening and was taking stock of the high brown roof and was getting used to the cool brown light when two other people came past outside on the turf. This time they were both young, a young man and a young woman. They were both in the prime of youth, or even in that season which precedes the prime of youth, the season before the smooth pink folds of the flower have burst their gummy case, when the wings of the butterfly though fully grown are motionless in the sun.

"Lucky it isn't Friday," he observed.

"Why? D'you believe in luck?"

"They make you pay sixpence on Friday."

"What's sixpence anyway? Isn't it worth sixpence?"

"What's 'it'—what d'you mean by 'it'"?

"O anything—I mean—you know what I mean."

Long pauses came between each of these remarks; they were uttered in toneless and monotonous voices.

'WHAT CAN SIX APPLES NOT BE?'

A small painting of seven apples by Paul Cézanne arrived in England in 1918. It sat in the hedge at the bottom of the farm lane leading up to Charleston, while the economist Maynard Keynes, who had acquired it from the sale of Edgar Degas' collection in Paris, carried the rest of his luggage up to the house. Duncan Grant ran down to fetch it. From then on at Charleston, where Keynes left the Cézanne for a period, and then in Roger Fry's studio, where it also lodged for a while, it became the object of intense scrutiny. 'What can six apples not be?' Woolf asked, miscounting the apples in her amazement at the attention this small painting attracted. She wanted to understand its power, for as her diary entry records, the apples seemed to get redder and rounder and greener, while the other paintings in the room seemed to recede, to pale into insignificance.

Up to this point, Woolf had been reluctant to respond to the impact of Post-Impressionism. The second of the two Post-Impressionist exhibitions, at which an entire room had been dedicated to the work of Henri Matisse, had left her growling: 'The Grafton [Galleries, home of the Second Post-Impressionist Exhibition], thank God, is over; artists are an abominable race. The furious excitement of these people all winter over their pieces of canvas coloured green and blue, is odious.'[20] And the news that Roger Fry was setting up the Omega Workshops, in order to let the new

excitement about colour, rhythm and form spill out of the frame and into the field of the decorative arts, produced a further wry comment. But among the handful of short stories that Woolf published in *Monday or Tuesday* (1921) is a piece entitled 'Blue and Green'. Its two short paragraphs contain no narrative, but evoke the sensations caused by these two colours through reference to objects and to nature.

Woolf's short stories earned her high praise from Roger Fry. After reading 'The Mark on the Wall' he wrote, 'You're the only one now Henry James has gone who *uses language as a medium of art*,[21] who makes the very texture of the words have a meaning and a quality really almost apart from what you are talking about.'[22] This remark, combined with his earlier question about texture and structure, may have contributed to her dissatisfaction with her second novel, *Night and Day*, despite its more flexible narrative and increased mastery of detail. It was after she had completed it that she wrote 'Modern Fiction', and there complained that 'the form of fiction most in vogue more often misses than secures the thing we seek'.

Opposite: *Still Life with Apples* by Paul Cézanne, *c.*1878. This painting appears to have begun Woolf's interest in Cézanne.

Above: *The Matisse Room, Second Post-Impressionist Exhibition* by Roger Fry, 1912.

Those two-and-thirty chapters 'more and more' cease 'to resemble the vision in our minds'.[23] In order to catch this elusive vision, the invention of a new kind of structure became a compelling necessity.

An author whom Woolf wanted to publish soon after the Hogarth Press began was Katherine Mansfield, the New Zealander who had settled permanently in London in 1908. 'Katherine Mansfield has dogged my steps for three years,' Woolf remarked to Strachey in 1916. 'I'm always on the point of meeting her, or of reading her stories, and I have never managed to do either.'[24] They met in February 1917. In April that year, Woolf called on Mansfield, then living in Old Church Street, Kensington, and asked for a story. In June Woolf invited Mansfield to a tête-á-tête dinner at Hogarth House, during which Katherine talked at length about her life and work. A further deepening of their friendship occurred after Mansfield submitted *Prelude* for publication and spent a weekend at Asheham with the Woolfs and Lytton Strachey, and Edward Garnett, the doyen of publishers' readers, who joined the party for one day. The small Regency house sat at the edge of a wood but in a landscape dominated by the magnificent bare slopes and declivities of the South Downs. The two women exchanged ideas about writing. 'It was good to have time to talk to you,' Mansfield wrote; 'we have got the same job, Virginia, and it is really very curious and thrilling that we should both, quite apart from each other, be after so very nearly the same thing.'[25]

Both wanted to go beneath the surface of family life or social behaviour; both were interested in what Woolf would call the 'lives of the obscure'; both wanted, in their different ways, to write with an economy, lyricism and speed that was modern; both were also outsiders. 'What a queer fate it is – always to be the spectator of the public,' wrote Woolf, 'never part of it. This is part of the reason why I go weekly to see K.M. at Hampstead, for there at any rate we make a public of two.'[26] Yet despite their shared endeavour, their friendship followed no steady course. Mansfield could be cold and unresponsive, perhaps owing to the difficulty of living with tuberculosis, which was first diagnosed in the winter of 1917–18. Their friendship was troubled by misunderstandings, jealousy, distrust and competition. Yet when Mansfield's *Prelude* came off the press, Woolf noted with satisfaction that it had 'the living power, the detached existence of a work of art'.[27]

Woolf's need for Mansfield gave her persistence. After Katherine married John Middleton Murry in May 1918 and moved to 2 Portland Villas in Hampstead, Woolf, when she did not visit, sent gifts of flowers and cigarettes, plus letters to which Katherine did not always reply. It could be argued that the best, if also the most painful, gift that Mansfield gave Woolf was her review of *Night and Day*, which appeared in the *Athenaeum* in November 1919. Having earlier admired *Kew Gardens*, she found much to praise, but the conventional mode irked her and she

Katherine Mansfield
photographed by
Adelphi Studios Ltd.,
60 Strand, London,
1913.

found it surprisingly Jane Austenish. Hence her conclusion, which stung: 'in the midst of our migration it makes us feel old and chill: we had never thought to look upon its like again.' Mansfield was abroad that winter for health reasons. On her return the following spring, she did not immediately contact Woolf. When visits were resumed, it took time to regain their former ease and for a mutual understanding to be revived. With the approach of another winter, Mansfield returned again to the South of France, this time to settle there, until she embarked on her final peregrinations. The two friends did not see each other again, but their association continued to occupy a special place in Woolf's mind, even after Mansfield's death in 1923. 'I am always thinking of things to say to you,' Woolf wrote in one of only two surviving letters by her to Katherine Mansfield. 'I sometimes think that though we're so different, we have the same difficulties.'[28] In turn, Katherine wrote from Menton-Garavan: 'You are the only woman with whom I long to talk work. There will never be another.'[29]

THE RUSSIAN CLASSICS

Mansfield's deep affection for Samuel Solomonovitch Koteliansky, a Ukrainian Jew and translator, makes it probable that his introduction to the Woolfs in 1917, soon after they set up the Hogarth Press, came from her. He dined with them in January 1918, along with the historian Arnold Toynbee and his wife Rosalind. In her diary, Virginia Woolf recorded their conversation, much of it Kot's, as he was nicknamed. He came again for dinner, this time in the company of the painter Mark Gertler, whom Woolf admired but thought unscrupulous. Kot, on the other hand, seemed to her very different, more in the style of 'solid lodging house furniture, but with an air of romance'.[30] Gertler's portrait of Koteliansky catches not only his likeness, including the way he always wore his hair *en brosse*, but also his characterful nature. Virginia Woolf once observed that his hands, though inches thick, were as hard as bone, and the clasp of his handshake so firm that it crushed the small bones in her own hand, and typified 'that dense, solid, concentrated man'.[31]

Owing to Koteliansky, Russian classics became a staple of the Hogarth Press. The press had quickly reached a turning point in 1919 with *Kew Gardens*, the demand for which obliged the Woolfs to employ a commercial printer for a second edition of 500 copies. They then did the same with 'The Mark on the Wall', printing it on its own in 1,000 copies. It was, therefore, just at the moment that the press was becoming a profitable business that Koteliansky approached Leonard with a copy of *Reminiscences of Leo Tolstoi*, which Maxim Gorky had just sent him, with the right to translate it into English. Koteliansky suggested that he and Leonard should work on its translation together, and Leonard agreed. What in effect this meant was that Kot filled a notebook with his own English translation, leaving a wide gap between each line so that Leonard could transpose colloquial Russian phrasing into the more stylised needs of good English prose. The book was published in July 1920 and sold so well that a second edition appeared the following year. Its success began an intense 'Russian' period for the Hogarth Press, resting on the collaboration between Kotelianksy and the Woolfs. Both Leonard and Virginia tried to learn Russian, but, like all Kot's English translators, their role was confined to correcting his English. Virginia began working with him in 1922, and her name is associated with Fyodor Dostoevsky's *Stavrogin's Confession*, a translation of three chapters from the 1871 novel *The Possessed*, which had been omitted from the original. Two other publications on which she worked with Kotelianksy were *Tolstoi's Love Letters* and *Talks with Tolstoi*, the latter co-authored by Kot with A.B. Goldweiser.

Her interest in Russian authors was another thing Woolf shared with Mansfield, whose short stories owe much to Anton Chekhov. Yet a more determining influ-

Samuel Solomonovitch Koteliansky by Mark Gertler, 1930.

ence on Woolf's third novel, *Jacob's Room* (1922), were those harsh comments that Mansfield had made public about *Night and Day*. Admittedly, this new novel had been preceded by another experimental short story, 'The Unwritten Novel', which scorns traditional narrative by satirising it. But what is immediately striking in *Jacob's Room* is the sprightly word painting, particularly in Woolf's description of, in her own words, 'the astonishing agitation and vitality of nature'. It upholds the biographer Claire Tomalin's remark that Woolf must have 'studied her friend's technique as well as pondering her review'.[32] In *Jacob's Room* there is almost no plot, and the central character, in several scenes, is defined by his absence, just as Woolf herself had been in Vanessa Bell's portrait of her in a deckchair. By now she was intensely aware of the example set by modern painting, which she later affirmed in her essay on Walter Sickert: 'painting and writing have much to tell each other, they have much in common'.[33]

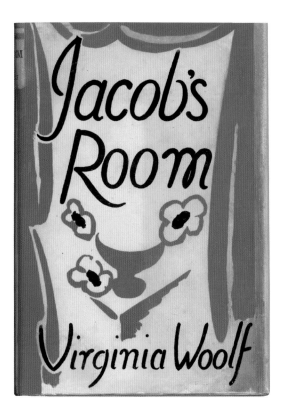

Jacob's Room by Virginia Woolf, Hogarth Press, 1922. Cover design by Vanessa Bell.

NOTES

1 From 'Pictures' (1925), in *The Essays of Virginia Woolf, Vol. 4: 1925–1928*, ed. Stuart N. Clarke (Hogarth Press, London, 1994), p.245.

2 Virginia Woolf, *Between the Acts* (Penguin, London, 1972), p.11.

3 Letter to Vanessa Bell, 12 May 1928, in *A Change of Perspective: The Letters of Virginia Woolf, Vol. 3: 1923–28*, ed. Nigel Nicolson, assisted by Joanne Trautmann (Hogarth Press, London, 1977), p.498.

4 *The Question of Things Happening: The Letters of Virginia Woolf, Vol. 2: 1912–1922*, ed. Nigel Nicolson, assisted by Joanne Trautmann (Hogarth Press, London, 1976), p.150.

5 A more detailed analysis of the excruciatingly slow and laborious method of printing in which the Woolfs engaged can be found in Hermione Lee, *Virginia Woolf* (Chatto & Windus, London, 1996), pp.363–4.

6 See Leonard Woolf, *Beginning Again: An Autobiography of the Years 1911–1918* (Hogarth Press, London, 1964), p.236.

7 The date on the title page of *Paris* is 1919, but it did not come out until 1920.

8 Mirrlees rejected Leonard Woolf's request to reprint it in an anthology in 1946.

9 See Louise DeSalvo, *Melymbrosia* (Cleis Press, Berkeley, California, 2000), which reconstructs from drafts an earlier version of *The Voyage Out*.

10 In *A Reflection of the Other Person: The Letters of Virginia Woolf, Vol. 4: 1929–1931*, ed. Nigel Nicolson, assisted by Joanne Trautmann (Hogarth Press, London, 1978), p.231.

11 *The Letters of Virginia Woolf, Vol. 2*, p.242.

12 Her comments on *Ulysses* in her Reading Notebooks (Berg Collection, New York Public Library) have been transcribed by Suzette Henke and are published in *The Gender of Modernism: A Critical Anthology*, ed. Bonnie Kime Scott (Indiana University Press, Bloomington, 1990), pp.642–5.

13 *The Letters of Virginia Woolf, Vol. 2*, p.551.

14 *The Diary of Virginia Woolf, Vol. 5: 1936–41*, ed. Anne Olivier Bell, assisted by Andrew McNeillie (Hogarth Press, London, 1984), pp.352–3.

15 *The Diary of Virginia Woolf, Vol. 1: 1915–19*, ed. Anne Olivier Bell (Hogarth Press, London, 1977), p.80.

16 *The Letters of Virginia Woolf, Vol. 2*, p.234.

17 *The Essays of Virginia Woolf: Vol. 4: 1925–1928*, ed. Andrew McNeillie (Hogarth Press, London, 1994), p.160.

18 *The Diary of Virginia Woolf, Vol. 2: 1920–1924*, ed. Anne Olivier Bell, assisted by Andrew McNeillie (Hogarth Press, London, 1978), p.199.

19 Ibid., pp.113–14.

20 *The Letters of Virginia Woolf, Vol. 2*, p.15.

21 My italics, not Fry's.

22 18 October 1918, Special Collections, University of Sussex.

23 *The Essays of Virginia Woolf, Vol. 3*, p.33.

24 *The Collected Letters of Katherine Mansfield, Vol. 1*, ed. Vincent O'Sullivan & Margaret Scott (Clarendon Press, Oxford, 1984), p.286.

25 *The Collected Letters of Katherine Mansfield, Vol. 1*, (1984), p.80.

26 *The Diary of Virginia Woolf, Vol. 1*, p.222.

27 Ibid., p.167, 12 June 1918.

28 13 September [1920?], Smith College, Massachusetts.

29 20 December 1920, Special Collections, University of Sussex.

30 *The Diary of Virginia Woolf, Vol. 1*, p.159.

31 *The Diary of Virginia Woolf, Vol. 2*, p.150.

32 Claire Tomalin, *Katherine Mansfield: A Secret Life* (Penguin, London, 1987), p.200.

33 *The Essays of Virginia Woolf, Vol. 6: 1933–1941*, ed. Stuart N. Clarke (Hogarth Press, London, 2011), p.43.

4 STREET HAUNTING AND NOVEL WRITING

In March 1924, the Woolfs moved back into the centre of London, having taken a ten-year lease from the Bedford Estate on 52 Tavistock Square in Bloomsbury. They took with them all the paraphernalia of the Hogarth Press and re-established it in their new basement. This also contained a billiard room, and a storeroom that doubled as Virginia's study. The ground floor and first floor of this five-storey house were sublet to a firm of solicitors, Dollman & Pritchard, leaving the upper two floors as living quarters for the Woolfs. This arrangement worked well for both parties and turned the house into a neat sandwich of business activities and private life.

New homes invite new arrangements. The Omega Workshops had closed in 1919, but the experience of putting their painterly skills to the service of interior decoration had led Vanessa Bell and Duncan Grant to send out, at Christmas 1922, an advertisement card (overleaf). It offered 'decorations domestic ecclesiastical theatrical'. Virginia might have had this in mind when, in February 1924, before moving into Tavistock Square, she told Vanessa that it was her aim to get them both to decorate the sitting room on the third floor. She paid £25 for this scheme, and might have had a say in the choice of motifs in each of the wall panels. The violin in the panel over the fireplace echoes the motif that Vanessa Bell had used in her woodcut (page 117) for Virginia's short story 'The String Quartet' in the 1921 collection *Monday or Tuesday*. The musical theme recurs, notably with the mandolin depicted on the fire-screen, which appears to have been part of the overall decorations. Designed by Duncan Grant, it was translated into tapestry by his mother Ethel Grant. A photograph of this screen and the fireplace shows a fan, almost certainly hand-decorated at the Omega, displayed fully open in the

Virginia Woolf at Garsington. Photographed by Lady Ottoline Morrell, June 1926.

Above: Card announcing Vanessa Bell and Duncan Grant's interest in receiving commissions for decorative schemes, Christmas 1922.

Right: The fireplace in the sitting-room at 52 Tavistock Square (1924), showing one of the wall decorations designed by Bell and Grant and the firescreen designed by Grant.

centre of the mantelpiece, with pottery on either side. Along the edge of the mantelpiece and around the two circles that ornament the two pillars on either side of the fireplace, is a dense row of dots, enlivening what might otherwise have been a dull piece of furnishing. Woolf evidently cherished these dots: when a need to repaint them arose, she wrote to her sister, asking how to make lavender blue, because the workman's initial attempt at recreating their charm had turned them a dull sea-green. Further pride in the overall interior is revealed by the willingness on the part of the Woolfs to permit *Vogue* magazine, in early November 1924, to include photographs of these decorations in an article on the decorative work of Bell and Grant, entitled 'Modern Interior Decoration' (page 14).

Modern is what Virginia Woolf now wanted to be. She had observed the economy and speed with which Katherine Mansfield assembled and dissolved scenes, or so her own experiments with 'the flight of time which hurries us so tragically along' in *Jacob's Room* suggest.[1] At Tavistock Square she was to produce work that would

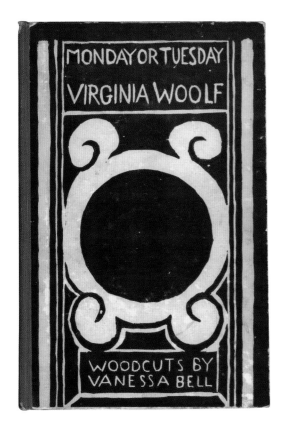

define her as one of the foremost modernist novelists of the twentieth century. Her interest in modernity was stimulated in no small part by London. 'London is enchanting,' she wrote in her diary soon after returning to live in Bloomsbury. 'I step out upon a tawny coloured magic carpet, it seems, and get carried into beauty without raising a finger.'[2] Her fourth novel, *Mrs Dalloway,* though begun at Hogarth House, was completed at Tavistock Square in October 1924 and published the following year. In this she takes her fictional character Clarissa Dalloway on a clearly defined walk from Westminster, through St James's Park, up Bond Street, across Cavendish Square and along Harley Street to Regent's Park, for, like Mrs Dalloway, she too delighted in the proximity of the city's constantly changing panorama – 'this, here, now, in front of her; the fat lady in the cab'.[3] But Woolf responded to the city at many levels, for, as she moved through it, the city's radical alterity seemed to effect a dissolution of the self, a sense that the boundaries between herself and the urban environment had been erased. In her essay 'Street Haunting: A London

Above, left: *Monday or Tuesday* by Virginia Woolf, Hogarth Press, 1921. Cover design by Vanessa Bell.

Above, right: 'The String Quartet' woodcut by Vanessa Bell, from *Monday or Tuesday,* 1921.

Mrs Dalloway by Virginia Woolf, Hogarth Press, 1925. Cover design by Vanessa Bell.

Adventure', first published in the *Yale Review* in 1927, she is led to ask, 'Is the true self neither this nor that, neither here nor there …?' The fluidity of movement offered by increasingly sophisticated systems of transport – the car, bus, Tube and train – enhanced her familiarity with many aspects of the city, with its street music, churning crowds and traffic, its river, beggars, statues, monuments; its music halls, publishing houses, theatres, concert halls and galleries, all offering rich sensory experiences and intellectual stimulation. The city also liberated her mind. 'One of these days,' she remarked in May 1924, 'I will write about London, and how it takes up the private life and carries it on, without any effort. Faces passing lift up my mind; prevent it from settling, as it does in the stillness of Rodmell.'[74]

The small Sussex village of Rodmell, which trickles down a road that leads nowhere, was the perfect antidote to the all-consuming heat of London. Here they found Monk's House, which, in 1919, Leonard bought at an auction in Lewes. It sat near the road, its front neatly weatherboarded, but its rear plain and bare, until many years later when Leonard added a conservatory. The Woolfs immediately had some internal partitions removed to create a more spacious feel to the ground floor, but a major attraction of this small house was the large stretch of land and small orchard that lay behind it, opening on to a view across water-meadows and fields to Mount Caburn. When, the following month, the contents of the house were

laid out on the lawn for another sale, Leonard bought apple trays, a lawn roller and many tools from the garden shed, for in time he was to create at Rodmell a garden of great beauty, composed of a series of 'rooms'. Even before the house had been made habitable, the Woolfs went down to Rodmell to work on the garden, Virginia noting in her diary the sense of satisfaction that comes from an entire day spent weeding. Monk's House replaced Asheham as their country retreat, but with greater permanence. No sooner had they acquired it than Virginia expressed the hope that they would live there till they died and be buried in the neighbouring graveyard of the parish church.

Back in London, however, she had more immediate concerns. The poet T.S. Eliot, who took pleasure in his annual visits to Rodmell, invited her to contribute to the *Criterion*, the literary magazine he had founded in 1922, and this pleased her, as did his approval of *Jacob's Room*, for it offset John Middleton Murry's stated conviction that this book had attempted the impossible. There were also parties to attend, which she no longer had to leave before they ended in order to take the District Line back to Richmond. Yet social life could still disconcert. She and Leonard enjoyed frequent dinner guests, as they had done at Hogarth House, among them Eliot, Mary Hutchinson – Clive Bell's mistress, Desmond MacCarthy, and the writer Osbert Sitwell, but their parties, so she told the painter and society

Rush Hour by Sybil Andrews, 1930. In this lithograph, Andrews neatly conveys the anonymity of the London Underground and the continuous movement up and down its escalators.

hostess Ethel Sands, were 'very small, very cheap', and she contrasted these with an aspect of London that she found 'rather frightening – so decorative, so vociferous, so smart too … I slink off into my own haunts, and feel refreshed by Bloomsbury and paralysed by Bond Street'.[5]

Feelings of ambiguity towards London extended to the Tube. While she lived in Bloomsbury, it was not a form of transport she used greatly, for she preferred to walk, to meander, or to sit upstairs in open-top buses so that she could feel the sun beating down on her neck. But her probing imagination was very aware that a large part of the city's life and movement now went on under the pavements and streets, and the presence of the Tube recurs in her novels. The writer Alexandra Harris has reminded readers of Woolf how the Tube's corporate image was 'forcefully promoted in the 1920s and 1930s as the epitome of speedy, stylish modernity'.[6] After Harry Beck redesigned the map of the London Underground in 1933, thus enabling the stations along the various routes and the connections between the nine different lines to be quickly identified, it became very much more widely used. Indeed, the Tube rapidly became the most popular and convenient method of traversing the city. Its signage benefited from the clear sans-serif typeface, specially produced for the London Underground by Edward Johnston; new stations were designed, in a functional yet Art Deco style, by Charles Holden; and Frank Pick, the assistant

Inside the illustration the following labels appear: SWAN & EDGAR'S, COUNTY FIRE OFFICE, MONICO, THE LONDON PAVILION, BOOKING HALL, ENTRANCE, REGENT STREET, BOVRIL, SCHWEPPES, SHAFTESBURY AVENUE, SHOW CASES, LOWER REGENT ST., Tobacco, fruit & Confectionery Stalls, Bookstall, Bookstall, SHOW CASES, Switch House, CIRCULATING AREA, MACHINERY FLOOR, ENTRANCE, ENTRANCE, CHANGE KIOSKS & AUTOMATIC BOOKING OFFICE, AUXILIARY BOOKING OFFICE, EAST BOUND, 5 ESCALATORS, 3 ESCALATORS (BAKERLOO), 3 ESCALATORS (PICCADILLY), PIPE SUBWAY, INTERCHANGE, PICCADILLY, STAIRCASE TO STREET, WEST BOUND, NORTH BOUND, SOUTH BOUND, D. MACPHERSON

manager and then managing director of the Underground Group, linked the Tube's practical function with contemporary art by commissioning bright, characterful, up-to-the-minute posters. Nevertheless, this miracle of engineering, organisation and corporate identity, resulting in a socially progressive infrastructure, aroused ambivalence in Virginia Woolf. Douglas MacPherson's 1928 drawing of the complex tunnels and connections underneath Piccadilly Circus, which she might have seen, hints at the complexity that is both reflected in and remarked upon in *The Waves* (1931) through the character of Jinny:

Piccadilly Circus Underground by Douglas MacPherson, 1928.

121

The Waves by Virginia Woolf, Hogarth Press, 1932. Cover design by Vanessa Bell.

Here I stand in the Tube station where everything that is desirable meets – Piccadilly South Side, Piccadilly North Side, Regent Street and the Haymarket. I stand for a moment under the pavement in the heart of London. Innumerable wheels rush and feet press just over my head. The great avenues of civilization meet here and strike this way and that. I am in the heart of life. But look – there is my body in that looking glass. How solitary, how shrunk, how aged! I am no longer young. I am no longer part of the procession. Millions descend those stairs in a terrible descent. Great wheels churn inexorably urging them downwards. Millions have died. Percival died. I still move. I still live. But who will come if I signal?[7]

The move is swift, from the recently built sub-surface booking hall fashionably designed by Holden, where Jinny feels momentarily in the heart of London, to an awareness of a 'terrible descent'. Woolf read Dante's *Divine Comedy* while writing *The Waves*, and the opening rings in his *Inferno* may have coloured her perception of the Tube, turning it into a frightening underworld. Watching the upright figures disappear soundlessly into the depths of the Underground, Jinny imagines 'the pinioned and terrible descent of some army of the dead downwards'.[8]

Here and elsewhere darkness shadows and pierces modernity. How could it not, in the aftermath of the First World War, when almost every family in Britain had been touched directly or indirectly by the loss of a relative, colleague, friend or acquaintance? Jacob Flanders in Woolf's 1922 novel is last glimpsed in Piccadilly by the Reverend Andrew Floyd, and through a car window by Clara Durrant in Long Acre, Covent Garden. His death is not described, but we learn of the strew of letters left behind in his room. 'Listless is the air in an empty room, just swelling the curtain; the flowers in the jar shift. One fibre in the wicker arm-chair creaks, though no one sits there.'[9] The elegy lies as much in these words as in the sound of his name, which his friend Bonamy cries helplessly from the window, while Jacob's mother wonders what should be done with an old pair of her son's shoes. The theme of loss is taken up again near the start of *Mrs Dalloway*, when Clarissa recollects how Lady Bexborough opened a bazaar with a telegram in her hand that contained news of her favourite son's death. References to 'the dead' recur in this novel, not least when a line of boy soldiers marches up Whitehall after laying a wreath at the Cenotaph, and when Doris Kilman observes people shuffling past the tomb of the Unknown Warrior in Westminster Abbey. In various ways, the Woolf scholar David Bradshaw argues, 'Woolf drives home her sense of the War's ongoing tragic aftermath, its refusal to leave hold of the living, the persistence of memory.'[10]

VITA AND VIRGINIA

After only two meetings with Virginia Woolf, the writer Vita Sackville-West had sufficient evidence to inform her husband Harold Nicolson of two things: 'she [Virginia] dresses quite atrociously', and that, nevertheless, she (Vita) had 'quite lost my heart' to this woman ten years her senior.[11] Clothes, of course, aren't everything, but, in the scheme of things, they matter, as Woolf herself knew, for on her second meeting with Vita she had replaced woollen orange stockings with yellow silk ones; and Vita had noticed.

Much has been written about the relationship between Virginia Woolf and Vita Sackville-West; about their shared interest in writing and their different social backgrounds. Vita fell quickly in love with Virginia, a fact that she admitted to her husband, himself homosexual, and with whom she maintained a deeply affectionate but open marriage. Virginia was initially more circumspect. Near the start of their friendship, at a dinner at which both Vita and Harold were present, she held up her father's Cambridge intellectual yardstick and found both of them wanting. She knew about Vita's 'Sapphism', and was intrigued by the fact that she had grown up at Knole, in a house, much of it fifteenth-century, with some 365 rooms. But their friendship did not unfold until after the Woolfs were settled at Tavistock Square. In 1925, Woolf published two books: *Mrs Dalloway* and the first of her two *Common Readers*, containing a selection of her essays. She also began mapping out the structure of *To the Lighthouse*. Vita expressed astonishment at how much Woolf did. 'You seem to combine in yourself at least six whole-time jobs: novelist, journalist, printer, publisher's reader, friend, relation. Each of these is an occupation in itself.'[12] This awareness must have put their romance in perspective, but even at

124

its most intense, it is likely to have been restrained. They spent few nights together and Woolf's extreme sensitivity and history of mental illness may have made Vita cautious. A more shallowing ingredient in their relationship was Vita's deviousness and promiscuity. For much of the time, Virginia was largely unaware that she was second if not third in line.

EMBRACING FASHION

Of more importance in connection with Woolf's modernity is the impact Vita had on Woolf's dress, appearance and self-presentation, all things that mattered increasingly as she grew in fame. Vita, usually pearl-hung, dressed in keeping with her class. Woolf, too, in the mid-1920s began to appear in public in elegant, sophisticated outfits, recognising in fashion a metonym for modernity and another means through which to explore identity.

The memory of George Duckworth's stern instruction – 'Go and tear it up!' – about the green dress that she'd had made of furnishing fabric when she was a young woman, filled her with a shame that she never forgot. Perhaps this is why, until now, she had dressed mostly in restrained styles and colours. Her attitude to clothes had been deeply disturbed when she first saw the outcome of Vanessa's designs for the Omega. 'My God! What colours you are responsible for!' she wrote to her sister after she saw her sister-in-law Karin Stephen wearing a skirt 'barred' with reds and yellows, a pea-green blouse and a gaudy scarf tied around her head. 'I shall retire', she vowed, 'into dove colour and old lavender, with a lace collar and lawn wristlets.'[13] But six months later she had taken the plunge. We find her writing to the Omega dressmaker in January 1917: 'I am coming to the Omega on Thursday, to be slightly altered.'

Woolf's interest in fashion was furthered in the 1920s by her association with *Vogue*. She enjoyed 'sweeping guineas off the *Vogue* counter'[14] in return for articles, as one editor after another – first Elspeth Champcommunal, then Dorothy Todd – sought to combine in the magazine high fashion with high art. In the May 1925 issue of *Vogue* a studio photograph of Woolf appeared, exquisitely dressed, if in a slightly demure fashion, and posed against a screen ornamented with birds and flowers (overleaf). Then, exactly a year later, she appeared again in *Vogue*, this time not in a contemporary outfit, but in a Victorian dress that had belonged to her mother (page 127). It is awkward in fit but the overall effect is defiantly backward-looking. The circumstances that led up to this excavation of matrilineal history are not known. But even if the idea did not originate with Woolf, her willingness to appear in this dress in a leading fashion magazine suggests that the agenda behind it had her full approval. The fact that she was at this time reinventing her mother, drawing on her memories of her person for the character Mrs Ramsay in *To the Lighthouse*, may be relevant. A twenty-first-century woman novelist might have turned such a photo-shoot to her advantage, using it to preview a forthcoming novel. But the paragraph of blurb that

Virginia Woolf
photographed by Maurice
Beck and Helen Macgregor
for *Vogue* magazine, late
May 1925.

accompanies this photograph simply summarises Woolf's career to date and does not mention the dress. There are in existence at least three photographs of Woolf in her mother's dress. In these, she is shown half length, with her arms resting on a table; three-quarter length; and, still seated, full length, making the entire dress visible. In all three there is a sense of divorce between the dress and the sitter. Yet it seems likely that Woolf approved this second photo-shoot because she wanted her commitment to the past, and the intergenerational exchange here imaged, to be held in conjunction with the earlier photograph and her pursuit of contemporaneity.

Because *Vogue* did not at this time have its own photography department, both sessions with Woolf had been shot by Maurice Beck and Helen Macgregor in their mews studio. Often present on these occasions was the young fashion editor Madge Garland, who would pose the model or advise on the angle of the shot, as she did on the occasion of Woolf's first appearance in *Vogue*. Garland was small, thin and

Virginia Woolf wearing her mother's dress photographed by Maurice Beck and Helen Macgregor for *Vogue* magazine, early May 1926.

immensely chic, and her appearance at any party immediately diverted attention. Because she was the partner of Dorothy Todd, and both had the good will of the famous chef Marcel Boulestin, they frequently entertained in his restaurant in Southampton Row, or persuaded him to serve food in their own home. The latter was the case when they invited Virginia Woolf to lunch to meet Sylvia Townsend Warner, who had just published her novel about witches, *Lolly Willowes* (1926). (Woolf asked how she knew so much about witches and was startled by the reply: 'Because I am one.')

Although Woolf consulted both Garland and Todd about clothes, it was Garland who brought to the fore what Woolf herself called 'frock-consciousness'.[15] She found Garland's charm excessive. Perhaps her one-liners – 'I like my children *prêt-à-porter* and my clothes made to measure' – were too self-conscious for Woolf's taste. But she would have recognised the accuracy of Lisa Cohen's description of Garland as

an 'intellectual devotee of haute couture'.[16] While lunching with Garland on one
occasion, Woolf admired her outfit, which had been designed by Nicole Groult,
the Parisian couturier and younger sister of the 'King of Fashion', Paul Poiret. It
consisted of a patterned two-piece dress and a plain-coloured long silk coat lined
with the same pattern as the dress and bordered in a similar manner to the wide-
brimmed hat. This outfit, as worn by Garland, was also admired by Cecil Beaton
in 1926, and in 1927, Edward (Teddy) Wolfe, who had briefly worked at the Omega
Workshops, painted her in it, though he left out the pattern on the dress. Her poise
and panache are conveyed through his assured, unfussy, elliptical treatment (much
of the white in the picture is, in fact, bare canvas). Madge Garland claimed that
one eye had been left unfinished because, before the sitting ended, they put on the
gramophone and started to dance.

With Woolf's permission, Garland commissioned from Groult a similar outfit
for Woolf, only in a different colour. Groult habitually brought her own fitter with
her when visiting London with a new collection, and this made possible the necessary fitting for final adjustments. The outfit, in Garland's opinion, made Woolf
look supremely elegant, and Virginia herself was greatly pleased. It was worn by
her on a visit to Garsington, the home of the society hostess Lady Ottoline Morrell,
in 1926 (pages 130–5). On this occasion Morrell took some fifteen photographs
of Woolf – standing, talking with others, or, at another moment, on her own, still
looking strikingly elegant while absorbed in the act of reading. 'If only', Woolf is
said to have remarked to Garland, 'you would always dress me I should have time
to write another book which I would dedicate to you!' If not actually verbatim, the
gist of this remark rings true.

NOVELIST AND ARTIST

As one novel by Virginia Woolf followed another during the 1920s, each was different from the last. Yet even *Orlando* (1928), her most light-hearted fictional
endeavour, inspired by her fascination with the romantic history that surrounded
Vita Sackville-West and her ancestral past, continues her central ambition: to
question and undo the formal constraints that had hitherto directed the writing of
personal, historical or fictional narrative, and to replace them with a different kind
of formal control. Teasing and playful *Orlando* may be, but the use of historical
and sexual mobility – the eponymous central character switches sex from man to
woman as he/she moves through the ages – continues to undermine the traditional
certainties of fiction and questions what determines identity.

The preface to *Orlando* satirises the self-importance and pomposity that often
creeps into biographers' acknowledgements. But one debt Woolf lists with accuracy
and respectful affection: 'To the unrivalled sympathy and imagination of Roger
Fry I owe whatever understanding of the art of painting I may possess.' It was a debt
directly related to her fiction, for there is much evidence that painting provoked

Maurice Bowra and
Virginia Woolf at
Garsington. Photographed
by Lady Ottoline Morrell,
June 1926.

Philip Nichols, Virginia
Woolf and Philip Morrell
at Garsington. Photo-
graphed by Lady
Ottoline Morrell,
June 1926.

Virginia Woolf at
Garsington. Photographed
by Lady Ottoline Morrell,
June 1926.

her, set her thinking. This is most clearly acknowledged in her essay 'Pictures', written in 1925. Here she pursues the argument that literature has always been receptive to the influence of the other arts. Of her own period, she writes:

> ... and now undoubtedly we are under the influence of painting. Were all modern paintings to be destroyed, a critic of the twenty-fifth century would be able to deduce from the works of Proust alone the existence of Matisse, Cézanne, Derain and Picasso; he would be able to say with those books before him that painters of the highest originality and power must be covering canvas after canvas, squeezing tube after tube, in the room next door.[17]

The example of modernist painting, with its balance of form, its use of echoes and repetitions to build a satisfying unity, suggested to Woolf that the novelist might also work with echoes and repetitions, with a balancing of incidents and characters, held together, not on the canvas, but in the mind. This is achieved, for instance, in *Mrs Dalloway* by the crossing of two different lives, those of Clarissa Dalloway and Septimus Warren, at one moment in time. Time itself becomes subject to a new conception: the Post-Impressionist painting – with its condensed or subjective recording of information, or the Cubist painting – with its use of fragmentation – suggested that the novelist might break up the more usual narrative sequence, which Woolf's experience of the cinema also upheld. 'My prime discovery so far,' Woolf wrote in her diary when composing *Mrs Dalloway*, is 'my tunnelling process, by which I tell the past by instalments as I have need of it.'[18] Still more important, perhaps, is the paring away of unnecessary detail and the sense, felt especially in *To the Lighthouse*, that every touch – as in a painting – must relate to the whole.

Woolf thought of dedicating *To the Lighthouse* to Roger Fry. She did not do so because, at the last minute, she doubted the book's worth. After reading the novel, he praised it highly. In her reply, she told how, meeting him one day in the street, she had felt the immensity of his personality, and had concluded that dedicating such a book to him was impossible. Her letter ends: 'Really therefore the non-dedication is a greater compliment than the dedication would have been .... What I meant was ... you have I think kept me on the right path, so far as writing goes, more than anyone – if the right path it is.'[19]

The path uncovered between *Night and Day* and *To the Lighthouse* pursues a steady increase in formal control and a gradual reduction of authorial intrusion. The formal control in *To the Lighthouse* reaches such a pitch that, as the writer Allen McLaurin argues,[20] when we put down this book, which ends with the painter Lily Briscoe's triumphant words, 'I have had my vision', we are invited not only to share her vision but to see the whole of the novel in a flash as we read the last words. Would Woolf have moved quite so firmly in this direction had she not enjoyed friendship with Roger Fry? As previously mentioned, it was he who first alerted her attention to texture and structure in her writing. Texture can be an important characteristic in a modernist painting; it serves to create a unity of touch. Cézanne, for instance, often made use of a fairly consistent hatched brushstroke, and spread his colour to the very edge of the canvas so that every inch is saturated, made resonant. Woolf acknowledged Cézanne's achievement but did so in a way that suggests she saw in his paintings a threat to the realm of language. 'No painter', she says of Cézanne, 'is more provocative to the literary sense, because his pictures are so audaciously and provocatively content to be paint, that, the very pigment they say, seems to challenge us, to press on some nerve, to stimulate, to excite.'[21]

Woolf conceived and wrote *To the Lighthouse* at a time when Bloomsbury's interest in Cézanne was at its height. In 1923 she read a biography of Cézanne. In 1924 Roger Fry, reviewing a Cézanne exhibition at the Goupil Gallery, London, praised his marrying of structure with a desire to realise a 'continuity of texture'.[22] In 1925, the year in which Woolf began work on *To the Lighthouse*, another Cézanne exhibition was held in London, at the Leicester Galleries. That same year Fry began writing a long article on the Cézannes in the Pellerin Collection which formed the basis for his book on Cézanne, which the Woolfs published in 1927, the same year that *To the Lighthouse* appeared.

In this novel Lily Briscoe paints a picture that is recognisably Post-Impressionist. What she is aiming for is something closely related to Cézanne's merging of texture and structure, his ability to combine a sense of flux with an underlying stability,

To the Lighthouse by Virginia Woolf, Hogarth Press, 1927. Cover design by Vanessa Bell.

for he famously announced that he wanted to do Poussin over again from nature.[23] He exemplified, in visual terms, Woolf's own concern with the need to create form that can incorporate disorder and the haphazardness of life. Almost certainly Woolf's perception of this quality in Cézanne came through Fry's writings. He once summed up Cézanne's achievement by means of a question: 'How, without missing the infinity of nature, the complexity and richness of its vibrations, how to build that solidly and articulately co-ordinated unity in which the spirit can rest satisfied?'[24] And here is Woolf, voicing Lily's thoughts on her painting: 'Beautiful and bright it should be on the surface, feathery and evanescent, one colour melting into another like the colours on a butterfly's wings; but beneath the fabric must be clamped together with bolts of iron. It was to be a thing you could ruffle with your breath; and a thing you could not dislodge with a team of horses.'[25]

'A good book', Woolf asserts in the non-fictional *A Room of One's Own* (1929), which immediately followed *To the Lighthouse*, 'leaves a shape on the mind's eye.' This phrase, with it suggestion of aesthetic unity and wholeness, reveals her to be an associate of Roger Fry, who spent much of his life searching out the aesthetic content in art, and whom she met one day in London's Charing Cross Road, carrying four or five books under his arm. Under his influence, she found herself blown into the nearest bookshop and made to lay out money on a book she did

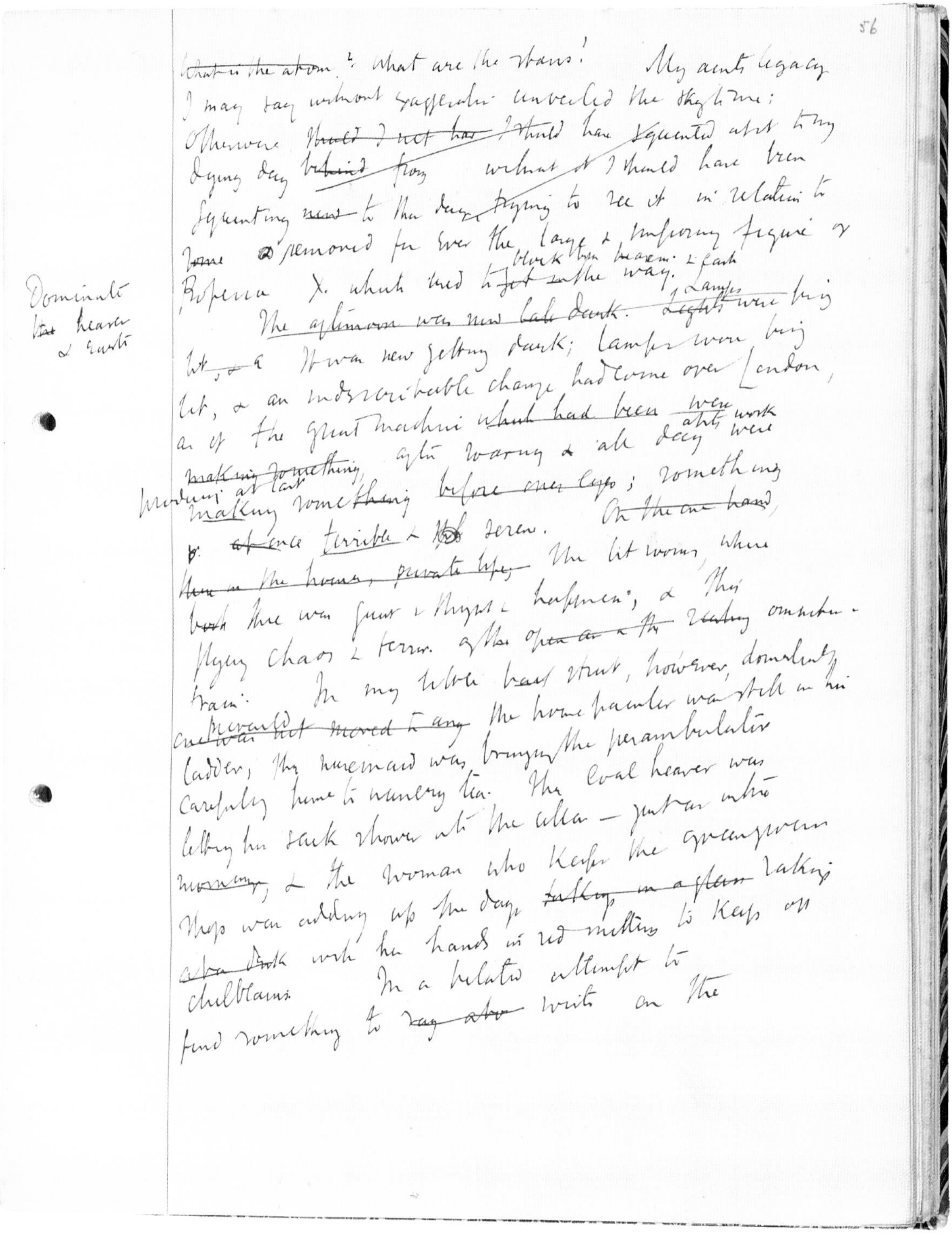
56

what are the stars? My aunt's legacy I may say without exaggeration unveiled the sky to me: Otherwise I should have squinted at it to my dying day from what I should have been squinting to the day trying to see it in relation to some removed for ever the large & imposing figure of Professor X. which used to block up heaven & earth the way.

Dominate heaven & earth

It was now getting dark; lamps were being lit, & an indescribable change had come over London, as if the great machine after working all day had at last were making something; something at once terrible & serene. the lit rooms, where there was fear & thought & happiness; & this chaos & terror. In my little back street, however, domesticity reigned. The house painter was still on his ladder, the nursemaid was bringing the perambulator carefully home to nursery tea. The coal heaver was letting his sack shower into the cellar — just as in the morning, & the woman who keeps the greengrocer shop was adding up the day's takings with her hands in red mittens to keep off chilblains. In a belated attempt to find something to write on the

Pages from the original manuscript of *A Room of One's Own* with the working title *Women in Fiction*, 1928–9. Above: A section of the manuscript that reflects her fascination with London. Opposite: Woolf here reflects on 'the androgynous mind', a term coined by Coleridge.

Otherwise one might find oneself hopelessly at sea.

Coleridge certainly did not mean by an androgynous, ^mind I
thought, going to the book case & passing before the many
books there, a mind that ~~has~~ has any ~~particular~~ special
sympathy with women: a mind that takes up their cause, or
~~anything~~ devotes ~~itself~~ to their interpretation.

The androgynous mind is less apt to ~~matter~~ ^t
make these distinctions than another. It is a mind
that is resonant; porous; that transmits emotion
~~from one~~ perpetually without impediment; that is
ceaselessly creative; ~~& with~~ incandescent; undivided.

In fact one goes back to Shakespeares mind as the
type of the androgynous, the man-womanly mind;
though it would be impossible to say what Shakespeare
thought of the other sex. ~~that he~~ ^It may indeed be ~~the~~ one of
~~condition of~~ the characteristics ^tendency of the ~~mind~~ fully
developed mind — a condition ~~which~~ now so much
harder to attain than it was then, I thought, ~~according~~
to the ~~modern~~ coming to books by living men; ^&
there pausing, uncertain what to open. ~~for~~ ~~these~~
~~under my hand~~, the No age can have been so
stridently ~~self~~ Sex-conscious as ours is I thought;
~~putting my hand upon one of~~ remembering these
innumerable books by men about women in the
British Museum. The Suffrage Campaign no
doubt was the cause of it. Nobody could
Grow up without thinking I am a man, & I am a
woman; & It ~~had to~~ must have roused
in men an extraordinary desire for self assertion;
it must have made them lay an emphasis

that it does not
think of sex
separately—

Nobody could
grow up now
without
thinky
I am a
man a
I am a
woman

not want; obliged to fix a date for a visit to his house and to accept an invitation to a play; left feeling, as her diary records, 'fairly overwhelmed – made to bristle all over with ideas, questions, possibilities'.[26] When he died in 1934 this fact, too, was recorded in her diary. 'Such a blank wall. Such a silence: such a poverty. How he reverberated.'[27]

A Room of One's Own by Virginia Woolf, Hogarth Press, 1929. Cover design by Vanessa Bell.

NOTES

1 Virginia Woolf, *Jacob's Room* (Penguin, London, 1992), p.134.

2 *The Diary of Virginia Woolf, Vol. 2: 1920–1924*, ed. Anne Olivier Bell, assisted by Andrew McNeillie (Hogarth Press, London, 1978), p.301.

3 Virginia Woolf, *Mrs Dalloway* (Oxford University Press, Oxford, 2008), p.8.

4 *The Diary of Virginia Woolf, Vol. 3: 1925–1930*, ed. Anne Olivier Bell (Hogarth Press, London, 1980), p.301.

5 *A Change of Perspective: The Letters of Virginia Woolf, Vol. 3: 1923–1928*, ed. Nigel Nicolson, assisted by Joanne Trautmann (Hogarth Press, London, 1977), p.112.

6 Alexandra Harris, 'Virginia Woolf Underground' in *Woolf and the City*, ed. Elizabeth Evans and Sarah Cornish (Clemson University Digital Press, South Carolina, 2010).

7 Virginia Woolf, *The Waves* (Oxford University Press, Oxford, 2008) p.160.

8 Ibid., p.161.

9 *Jacob's Room*, p.155.

10 David Bradshaw, 'Introduction' in Virginia Woolf, *Mrs Dalloway* (Oxford University Press, Oxford, 2008), p.xii.

11 19 December 1922, quoted in Nigel Nicolson, *Portrait of a Marriage* (Weidenfeld & Nicolson, London, 1983), p.119.

12 11 October 1925: *The Letters of Vita Sackville-West to Virginia Woolf*, ed. Louise DeSalvo and Mitchell A. Leaska (Virago, London, 1992), p.98.

13 *A Question of Things Happening: The Letters of Virginia Woolf, Vol. 2: 1912–1922*, ed. Nigel Nicolson, assisted by Joanne Trautmann (Hogarth Press, London, 1976), p.11.

14 *The Diary of Virginia Woolf, Vol. 3*, p.33.

15 Ibid., p.12.

16 Lisa Cohen, 'Madge Garland and the Work of Fashion', *GLQ: A Journal of Lesbian and Gay Studies*, Vol. 11, issue 3, pp.371–90. Quoted in Jane Garrity, 'Virginia Woolf and Fashion', in *Virginia Woolf and the Arts* (Edinburgh University Press, Edinburgh, 2010), p.203.

17 'Pictures' (1925), in *The Essays of Virginia Woolf, Vol. 3: 1919–1924*, ed. Andrew McNeillie (Hogarth Press, London, 1994), p.243.

18 *The Diary of Virginia Woolf, Vol. 2*, p.272.

19 *The Letters of Virginia Woolf, Vol. 3*, p.385.

20 See Allan McLaurin, *Virginia Woolf: The Echoes Enslaved* (Cambridge University Press, Cambridge, 1973), p.206.

21 *The Essays of Virginia Woolf, Vol. 4: 1925–1928*, ed. Stuart N. Clarke (Hogarth Press, London, 1994), pp.244–5.

22 *Burlington Magazine,* Vol. XLV, December 1924, pp.311–12.

23 Nicolas Poussin (1594–1665) was a highly influential artist whose classical perfection Cézanne greatly admired.

24 Roger Fry, *Characteristics of French Painting* (Chatto & Windus, London, 1932), pp.144–5.

25 Virginia Woolf, *To the Lighthouse*, ed. David Bradshaw (Oxford World Classics, Oxford, 2008), p.141.

26 *The Diary of Virginia Woolf, Vol. 1: 1915–1919*, ed. Anne Olivier Bell (Hogarth Press, London, 1977), p.134.

27 *The Diary of Virginia Woolf, Vol. 4: 1931–1935*, ed. Anne Olivier Bell, assisted by Andrew McNeillie (Hogarth Press, London, 1978), p.235.

5 'THINKING IS MY FIGHTING'

The Virginia Woolf we encountered in the 1920s is primarily associated with the history of modernism, owing to her involvement with the Hogarth Press and experiments with novel-writing. In the next decade, a different Virginia Woolf comes to the fore. Like other intellectuals, she finds herself politicised by the events of the 1930s. Her concern about the subjection of women within the society of her day deepens. The progress of her writing is not straightforward. She conceives of a new genre, the 'novel-essay', in which fictional scenes alternate with historical commentary, but it proves abortive. At one point, in order to cool her mind, she throws off *Flush* (1933), a biography of the poet Elizabeth Barrett Browning's dog, who witnesses the important events in his owner's life. Woolf's expert knowledge of doggish behaviour owed much to the puppy that Vita Sackville-West had given her. *Flush* is, nevertheless, a surprising follow-up to *The Waves*.

The texture of her life flows through her diaries and fills many of her letters. She is fascinated and appalled by the ceremony that attends the marriage of Rachel MacCarthy to David Cecil, and is moved to tears at the annual Labour Party Conference at Brighton, when George Lansbury, Leader of the Labour Party, resigns in the wake of Ernest Bevin's attack on his policy regarding sanctions on Italy. With Leonard, she made several trips abroad during the inter-war period – to France, Italy, Greece, Holland and Germany, but it was the beauty, melancholy and poverty of Ireland that touched her deeply, and where, in conversation with those she met, she admired the stories she was told: 'the flowing, yet formed sentences, the richness & ease of the language; the lay out, dexterity and adroitness of the arrangement'.[1] Language, of course, was her own medium, and the difficulties

Virginia Woolf photographed by Man Ray at his temporary London studio at the offices of the Lund Humphries publishing house, 27 November 1934.

and exhilaration she experienced when composing are logged in her diaries, along with her ideas and plans for books and articles. Her concern for her reputation is very much to the fore, for her vaulting ambition as a writer had, if anything, intensified with age. She observes in one article: 'When we read the letters of Keats, the diary of the Goncourts, the letters of Lamb, the casual remarks of that unfashionable poet Tennyson, we feel that, waking or sleeping, these men never stopped thinking about literature. It is kneaded into the stuff of their brains. Their fingers are dyed in it. Whatever they touch is stained with it. Whatever they are doing their minds filled up involuntarily with some aspect of their absorbing question.'[2] Woolf, too, belonged to this tribe.

She continued to multi-task, and among the calls on her attention was the biography of Roger Fry, which, after his death in 1934, his sister Margery had persuaded her to write. The necessary painstaking research irked her, but at the same time this task intrigued her and provoked fresh thought about the nature of this genre.[3] She also broadcasted on BBC radio on three occasions. Only one of these recordings still exists: 'Craftsmanship', made in 1937, was part of the series *Words Fail Me*, a title she merely acknowledged in passing. Her focus was entirely on words, which, she argues, 'survive the changes and chops of time longer than any other substance … they are the truest'.[4] What then, she asks, is the proper use for words?

> Words, English words, are full of echoes, of memories, of associations – naturally. They have been out and about, on people's lips, in their houses, in the streets, in the fields for so many centuries. And that is one of the chief difficulties in writing them today – that they are so stored with meanings, with memories, that they have contracted so many famous marriages. The splendid word 'incarnadine', for example – who can use it without remembering also 'multitudinous seas'?[5] …. Words belong to each other, although, of course, only a great writer knows that 'incarnadine' belongs to 'multitudinous seas'… Our business is to see what we can do with the English language …. How can we combine the old words in new orders so that they survive, so that they create beauty, so that they can tell the truth? That is the question.[6]

Her passion for words was inevitably a factor in her and Leonard's continuing involvement with the Hogarth Press. For many years they were the only readers of the manuscripts submitted. But the press was changing: the success of *Orlando* in 1928, followed by the even greater success in 1930 of Vita Sackville-West's *The Edwardians,* which sold 30,000 copies, meant that the Woolfs now had a small business, three typists, bookkeepers and a manager in their home, and were publishing twenty to thirty books a year. They were keen on socio-political or literary pamphlets, even though booksellers did not like them, and produced nearly two dozen series in this format, including one entitled 'Living Poets', in which Frances Cornford was included, Woolf no longer holding to the cynical views she expressed during her breakdown in 1915. But although the press was to publish Christopher Isherwood's Berlin stories, it was no longer at the forefront of modernist developments, and by 1933 Woolf recognised that something had been lost. Thus, in 1938, when a former manager, John Lehmann, returned to the press after some years abroad, she agreed to sell him her half-ownership of it, which Lehmann thereafter ran as the managing partner, with part-time assistance from his co-partner Leonard.

The interest at the Hogarth Press in anti-imperialist and socio-political subjects and in books that reach across divisions created by class, education and nationality, justifies the term 'democratic intellectual' which Melba Cuddy-Keane has used of Woolf.[7] It is a term that also relates to her commitment to the common reader and to essay writing which, Andrew McNeillie argues, is 'democratic in spirit: uncanonical, inquisitive, open, and unacademic'.[8] Woolf, herself, prepared two collections of her essays for publication in her lifetime, both called *The Common Reader*, and published in 1925 and 1932. The form of her attention was also democratic in that the material for her novels is drawn from many aspects of society, yet her social reach was limited, in part owing to pressures on her time. When news reached the Woolfs that Miss West, one of the best managers they had employed at the press, was dying of pneumonia, Virginia experienced regret:

> A melancholy walk with L. in the rain. The usual thoughts: and this too; that I was too aloof, & never friendly eno', never asked her to dine. I must conquer this aloofness if I possibly can. So little one can do; but at least do it if possible. Such a mute relationship. I pass her room, and think I might have gone in; and now never shall.[9]

'DEATH IS THE ENEMY'

The presence of death, a significant feature in her teenage years and early adulthood, had once again come to the fore. Roger Fry's death had been preceded by that of Lytton Strachey in 1932 and, in turn, Strachey's death had brought on Dora Carrington's suicide. While in Ireland in 1934, the Woolfs discovered an obituary of George Duckworth in *The Times*. Virginia, after listing all the treats he had made possible, noted that his passing took away her childhood. Her unequivocal sense of loss contains no hint that his behaviour was ever untoward or that anything remiss ever happened between them. But sitting on her bed in a windy seaside hotel, waiting for dinner, she had 'this usual sense of time shifting & life becoming unreal, so soon to vanish while the world will go on millions upon millions of years'.[10]

Leonard Woolf claimed that death, and the contemplation of death, were never far from the surface of his wife's mind. It is a significant factor in most of her novels, nowhere more so than in *The Waves*. 'The complexity of things becomes more close,' remarks Bernard, the character who is gifted with the lengthy monologue that closes the novel. With this monologue in mind, Woolf wondered if she could make prose move 'from the chuckle & the babble to the rhapsody'.[11] In the course of this long passage, Bernard faces the dissolution of the self. He wonders how 'to describe the world seen without a self', and at one point knocks on the table to assure himself of its fixity and reality. 'Heaven be praised for solitude,' he volunteers, and momentarily finds contentment. 'Let me sit here for ever with bare things, this coffee cup, this knife, this fork, things in themselves, myself being myself.' But the restaurant is closing and the head waiter implies he must leave. Tired and spent, he re-enters the street, and momentarily experiences a renewal of desire. Like a young man on a horse, he sees the final enemy advancing. The book ends: 'It is death. Death is the enemy. It is death against whom I ride with my spear couched and my hair flying back like a young man's, like Percival's, when he galloped in India. I strike spurs into my horse. Against you I will fling myself, unvanquished and unyielding, O Death!'

These were by no means Woolf's last words, but they aptly sum up her philosophy towards life, and the final sentence was to be used by Leonard Woolf on a memorial to her in the garden at Monk's House.

A ROOM OF ONE'S OWN

In 1934 Woolf attended a preview of Man Ray's photographs, at the invitation of his fellow American Edward McKnight Kauffer. The following day, 27 November 1934 (not 1935, as is often stated), Virginia Woolf, aged 52, sat for her portrait to Man Ray in London. Three known photographs resulted from this session, but the one that best conveys her powerful mind and her 'daunting social presence', which turned heads at parties,[12] is the profile portrait where her head and shoulders are framed against a dark background (page 144). This is the woman who, in 1940, rightly claimed, 'My thinking is my fighting.'[13]

Connected with her growing interest in feminist thought is her friendship with the composer and suffragist Dame Ethel Smyth. This friendship had begun in 1930, when Virginia was forty-eight and Ethel seventy-two. Woolf's biographers write about this relationship with incredulity, not just because of the difference in age but also because of the strident differences between their two characters. The biographer Hermione Lee, describing the extent to which Smyth's whole way of life was still defined by the 1890s, estimates that Woolf must have found her late Victorian associations 'stuffy and antediluvian'. Nevertheless, this battle-axe of a composer, who had written 'March of the Women' in Holloway Jail and is said to have conducted it with a toothbrush through the bars of her prison window; this golf-loving rumbustious women with red cheeks, a battered moleskin coat and a hat that a hotel proprietor had pinned for her into the shape of a tricorne; this egocentric, loquacious woman who poured out intimate details about her professional and private life, and who announced that friendship with Virginia would fructify her final years and enable her to sing her 'Nunc dimittis', won Woolf over. How could she not? She had, Woolf noted, 'enormous eagerness' but also 'a quality I adore' – bravery.[14]

What brought them together was *A Room of One's Own*. This book is still widely regarded as having something to contribute to today's ongoing debate about

feminism, and appears in booklists for courses on Women's Studies. It is the product of deep reflection on women, society, literature and on what matters in life, yet is delivered in a light, gently ironical, conversational tone, which in no way belittles Woolf's purpose, for the adroit argument is a bid for freedom. 'But, you may say,' the book begins as if in mid-conversation. At its heart is a simple materialist claim – that in 1929 (the year the book was published) a woman needed £500 a year and a room of her own in order to write. Imaginative fiction, Woolf argues,

> … is not dropped like a pebble upon the ground, as science may be; fiction is like a spider's web, attached ever so lightly perhaps, but still attached to life at all four corners. Often the attachment is scarcely perceptible; Shakespeare's plays, for instance, seem to hang there complete by themselves. But when the web is pulled askew, hooked up at the edge, torn in the middle, one remembers that these webs are not spun in mid-air by incorporeal creatures, but are the work of suffering human beings, and are attached to grossly material things, like health and money and the houses we live in.[15]

In 1931, only two years after *A Room of One's Own* was published, Woolf began filling three scrapbooks with press cuttings, flyers and photographs that were relevant to her deepening interest in the position of women in society. In the same way that her paper on 'Women and Fiction', delivered at two Cambridge colleges, Girton and Newnham, had led to *A Room of One's Own*, so her willingness to talk on 'Professions for Women', at the request of Philippa (Pippa) Strachey, Lytton's sister and secretary of the National Society for Women's Service, had encouraged her attempt at a 'novel-essay'. As mentioned, Woolf abandoned this project (published posthumously as *The Pargiters* in 1978), but the work around it contributed to the genesis and evolution of her historical novel *The Years* (1937) – an attempt to revive the Victorian novel in a new way – and *Three Guineas* (1938), both of which draw on the contents of the scrapbooks.[16] In these can be found a wide range of information, but most of it, in some way, touches on the position of women. For instance, among the many cuttings are Hitler's instruction that women's duties should be limited to the three Ks – *Kinder, Küche, Kirche* (children, kitchen, church), as well as the 1937 New Year's Honours list, which included the names of 147 men and only 7 women.

Three Guineas is more vehement and far-reaching than *A Room of One's Own*, and startlingly prescient in relation to today's world, with its widespread warfare, aggression and recurrent incidences of rape and other forms of violence towards women and children. Woolf's starting point is again the restrictions imposed in her day on women's education and employment that shut women out of many professions and leave them, she observes, relatively powerless and the weakest of all classes in the state. What made this situation additionally frustrating, at a time when fascism versus democracy had become the issue of the day, was the question Woolf received in the post: 'How, in your opinion, are we to prevent war?' How indeed, given the restrictions on women's position in society? Woolf also received through the post

photographs of children killed during the Spanish Civil War.[17] The question about how to prevent war recurs in *Three Guineas*, as do references to the photographs of dead children. The latter appear to have been sent to her as part of the propaganda effort on the part of the Spanish government. They and other things confirmed Woolf in her disturbing belief that there was a connection between the rigidity of patriarchal societies and the destructiveness of war. This sliding scale is at its most extreme in *Three Guineas* in her discussion of St Paul: owing to his love of the law and of subjection, Woolf identifies him as 'the virile or dominant type, so familiar at present in Germany, for whose gratification a subject race or sex is essential'.[18]

WAR

Her nephew Julian Bell's involvement with Spain tied Woolf into this war at a personal level. In 1935 he had been offered a post as professor of English at the National University of Wuhan at Hankow, and had left for China that summer. In recognition of the deep bond of affection between Julian and his mother, Duncan Grant

Above, left: *The Years* by Virginia Woolf, Hogarth Press, 1937. Cover design by Vanessa Bell.

Above, right: 'This is what Fascism Means!', International Brigade pamphlet, 30 October 1936. 'As we listen to the voices we seem to hear an infant crying in the night, the black night that now covers Europe, and with no language but a cry, Ay, ay, ay … But it is not a new cry, it is a very old cry.' (*Three Guineas*, p.269)

151

Opposite: Julian Bell,
*c.*1935.

Above: Vanessa Bell by
Duncan Grant, *c.*1935. In 1935
Julian Bell took this portrait
of his mother with him when
he took up a university
appointment in China.

had painted a portrait of Vanessa for him to take with him (page 153). Earlier that year, Julian had edited a collection of essays written by conscientious objectors, *We Did Not Fight*. In the introduction he had admitted that, despite the book's pacifist stance, there were situations that called for force. But this tentative compromise hardened into something very different once the Spanish Civil War began. He had a good knowledge of military strategy and, after reading about the Spanish government's defeats and the British government's policy of non-intervention, he decided to leave China and enlist in the International Brigade. In an exchange of letters, he accused Woolf of being part of the generation whose inaction has allowed fascism to grow. He now believed: 'We have to abandon what is good, a free, tolerant, humane culture, and follow what is evil: violence, compulsion, cruelty. We must do this because this is the rational choice of the lesser evil, because only by doing so can we hope to avoid complete, extinguishing disaster.'[19]

In February 1937 he sailed to Marseilles and went to see the writers Charles and Marie Mauron, then still living in the traditional stone house they had bought jointly with Roger Fry at St-Rémy-de-Provence. Julian had asked Vanessa to come over and meet him there, as he intended to go straight to Spain from France. Vanessa had learnt of his desire to enlist after hearing the news that Frances Cornford's son John had been killed on the Córdoba front in December 1936. The Woolfs, knowing this, looked in on Vanessa Bell in her Fitzroy Street studio. 'Nessa was in one of her submerged moods on Monday when we went in,' Virginia wrote. 'Always that extraordinary depth of despair.'[20]

Vanessa begged Julian to return briefly to Charleston in Sussex, the country home of the Bloomsbury Group, where they could talk in peace and quiet. Mauron upheld her request, and Julian arrived back in England. A family reunion took place at Charleston on 13 March 1937 at which the Woolfs were present. Although no attempt was made that evening to change Julian's mind, he was eventually dissuaded from enlisting and instead applied for a job as an ambulance driver with Spanish Medical Aid. After he left for Spain, Vanessa and her younger son, Quentin, together with Leonard and Virginia, sat on the platform of the Albert Hall, with other artists, writers and performers, in support of an event organised by the National Joint Committee for Spanish Relief. Its chief purpose was to raise money for Basque refugee children, many of whom had been orphaned in the conflict. Quentin had attempted to secure the presence of Pablo Picasso, but he did not appear. Instead he donated a drawing of a weeping woman to be sold that evening in aid of the cause. This was not the only time that Woolf lent her support to the Spanish cause. In October 1938, when Picasso's *Guernica* and sixty-seven studies for it arrived at the New Burlington Galleries in London, Virginia Woolf's name was listed in the catalogue among the patrons and sponsors.

Three weeks after the Albert Hall event, on 20 July 1937, Vanessa was in her studio when the telephone rang. It was heard by George Rivers, a wood-carver in the workshop below, who had just posted to Julian the packing case he had made

Weeping Woman by Pablo Picasso, 1937. Donated by Picasso to the National Joint Committee for Spanish Relief.

155

NEW BURLINGTON GALLERIES
BURLINGTON GARDENS — LONDON W.1

VISIT

the

EXHIBITION

of

PICASSO'S

G
U
E
R
N
I
C
A

with over

60

preparatory paintings
sketches and studies
for the composition.

ENTRANCE 1/3

OCTOBER 4TH—29TH
DAILY 10 a.m. — 5.30 p.m.

GUERNICA
EXHIBITION

PATRONS

Gerald BARRY, Esq.
Fenner BROCKWAY, Esq.
The Rt. Hon. the Viscount
CECIL of CHELWOOD, P.C., K.C.
Sir Peter CHALMERS MITCHELL,
C.B.E., LL.D., F.R.S.
Douglas COOPER, Esq.
Hugh Sykes DAVIES, Esq
Professor Bonamy DOBREE
George EUMORFOPOULOS, Esq., F.S.A.
E. M. FORSTER, Esq.
Victor GOLLANCZ, Esq.
Ashley HAVINDEN, Esq.
A. P. HERBERT, M.P.
Julian S. HUXLEY, Esq. D.Sc., F.R.S
E. McKNIGHT KAUFFER, Esq.
David LOW, Esq.
D. MITRINOVITCH, Esq.
Mrs. Naomi MITCHESON
P. J. NOEL BAKER, M.P.
The Rt. Hon. Lord NOEL-BUXTON, P.C.
Harry POLLITT, Esq.
Miss Eleanor RATHBONE, M.P.
Ruthven TODD, Esq.
Professor TREND
Peter WATSON, Esq.
Mrs. Virginia WOOLF

ORGANISING COMMITTEE

Chairman: Wilfrid ROBERTS, M.P.
Vice-Chairman: Herbert READ, Esq.
The Rt. Hon. the Earl of LISTOWEL
Hon. Treasurer: Roland A. PENROSE, Esq.
Hon. Organiser: E. L. T. MESENS, Esq.
Hon. Secretary: Mrs. Sybil STEPHENSON

IN AID OF THE NATIONAL
JOINT COMMITTEE FOR SPANISH RELIEF

Poster for Picasso's
Guernica exhibition at New
Burlington Galleries, 1938.

and that Vanessa had filled with parcels. The cry that followed was something he never forgot, for the call had brought news of Julian's death.

It was nine days before Vanessa could be moved to Charleston. She had suffered a complete breakdown and for some days was beyond reach. She was given somnifene to help her sleep and was gradually persuaded to eat. The person whose love and persistence first reached her was that of her sister. Woolf came daily. Four years later Vanessa wrote to Vita Sackville-West: 'I remember all those days after I heard about Julian lying in an unreal state and hearing her voice going on and on keeping life going as it seemed when otherwise it would have stopped.'[21] At Charleston she lay on a bed placed in a corner of the studio, near the doors that opened on to the garden. Again Virginia came daily. In the loosened-up state that tragedy brings in its wake, Woolf was able to admit what she had often been obliged to curb or conceal. 'Why is it I never stop thinking of you, even when walking in the marsh this afternoon …. Lord knows I can't say what it means to come into the room and find you sitting there.'[22] But another person Woolf went on talking and arguing with on her walks across the marsh was Julian, for their disagreements over fighting and pacifism had never been resolved.

UNCONSCIOUS MEMORY TRACES

Woolf's final book, *Between the Acts*, was begun in 1938 and was undergoing revision when the Blitz began in 1940. 'I will continue – but can I?' Woolf asked herself.[23] It was hard to create amid destruction, and with bomber planes flying nightly over Rodmell. Woolf's need for anonymity, her interest in the lives of the obscure, in humdrum situations and everyday events, were precisely the things now under threat. Her curiosity and interest in life did not lessen, for she held fast to Henry James's injunction – 'observe perpetually'.[24] She and Leonard, aware of how Jews had been treated in other countries, discussed the possibility of using their car and garage at Rodmell as a means for suicide, should Hitler decide to invade Britain. As their names were included in the Black Book, compiled for Hitler by his head of counter-espionage Walter Schellenberg, they would have been arrested at the first opportunity following an invasion.

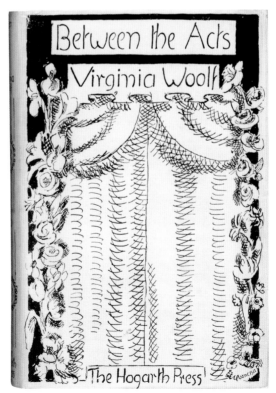

Between the Acts by Virginia Woolf, Hogarth Press, 1941. Cover design by Vanessa Bell.

Leonard, a strong supporter of the League of Nations and adviser to the Labour Party on international relations, had recognised that an almighty smash lay ahead in March 1936, when Hitler sent his troops into the de-militarised zone of the Rhineland. Such aggression made some of the Woolfs' activities, such as their membership of For Intellectual Liberty, the British equivalent to the French anti-fascist intellectual organisation, the Comité de Vigilance, seem very small. 'It's odd', Virginia Woolf wrote at this time, 'how near the guns have got to our private life again. I can quite distinctly see them and hear their roar, even though I go on, like a doomed mouse, nibbling at my daily page.'[25]

Much of the energy that she poured into *Between the Acts* – originally called *Pointz Hall* – was stimulated by the release she felt when she turned aside from the laborious nature of her work on the Roger Fry biography. Everything takes place in this short novel in the course of twenty-four hours. It is set largely on the estate of a country house where an historical pageant is to be performed on a summer day at a time when everyone is aware that the country is heading for war. 'History is now and England,' Eliot wrote contemporaneously in 'Little Gidding'. Woolf is saying something very similar, as she interleaves the past and present, history and prehistory, the national and the local. The novel is strewn with interruptions, as well as 'orts, scraps and fragments', and at the same time enlivened by singing, music, chatter, quotations, ditties, the bellowing of cows and the noise of overhead aeroplanes. It is less about individual life than common experience; and if anything is to be salvaged from these fragments during and after the forthcoming war, it is the vitality and continuity of collective existence and memory. The literary scholar Gillian Beer concludes that Woolf 'concurs with Freud's observation that individual and masses "retain an impression of the past in unconscious memory traces" and "there probably exists in the mental life of the individual not only what he has experienced himself, but also what he brought with him at birth, fragments of phylogenetic origin, an archaic heritage".'[26]

Woolf read Sigmund Freud's *Moses and Monotheism*, from which the above quotations are drawn, soon after it came out in March 1939, for the Hogarth Press was committed to publishing the standard English edition of Freud's writings in James Strachey's translation. On 28 January 1938, four months after Freud had arrived in London from Vienna, the Woolfs had visited him at 20 Maresfield Gardens in Hampstead. He was waiting for them in his consulting room, lined with books and his collection of antiquities and small figurines. Woolf, though seated on a chair and not Freud's couch, felt like a patient. She noticed how shrunken and old Freud looked and that talk was difficult. The cancer in Freud's jaw and throat made speaking painful. The conversation touched on Hitler and the war, and may have been helped by Freud's daughter Anna, who was present, as was one of his sons. At one point Freud ceremoniously gave Woolf a narcissus.

After reading *Moses and Monotheism*, Woolf turned again to Freud in December 1939. 'Began reading Freud last night; to enlarge the circumference. To give my brain

Sigmund Freud at his home,
20 Maresfield Gardens,
Hampstead, 1939.

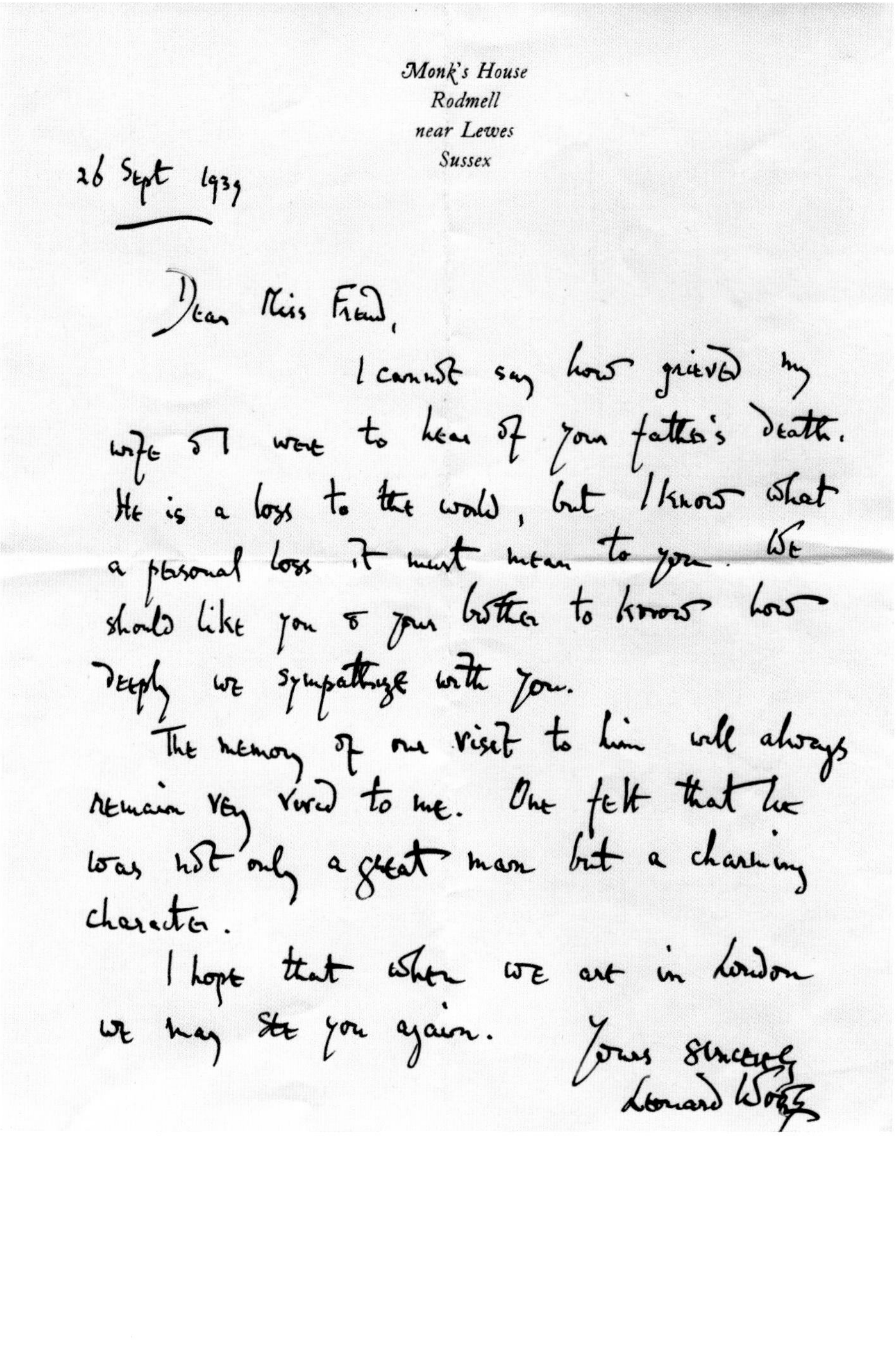

Letter from Leonard to Freud's daughter Anna, 26 September 1939. Letter reads: Dear Miss Freud, I cannot say how grieved my wife and I were to hear of your father's death. He is a loss to the world, but I know what a personal loss it must mean to you. We should like you and your brother to know how deeply we sympathise with you. The memory of our visit to him will always remain very vivid to me. One felt that he was not only a great man but a charming character. I hope that when we are in London we may see you again. Yours sincerely Leonard Woolf

> Monk's House
> Rodmell
> near Lewes
> Sussex

26 Sept 1939

Dear Miss Freud,

I cannot say how grieved my wife & I were to hear of your father's death. He is a loss to the world, but I know what a personal loss it must mean to you. We should like you & your brother to know how deeply we sympathise with you.

The memory of our visit to him will always remain very vivid to me. One felt that he was not only a great man but a charming character.

I hope that when we are in London we may see you again.

Yours sincerely
Leonard Woolf

a wider scope: to make it objective; to get outside. Thus defeat the shrinkage of age.'[27] Freud's use of the term 'ambivalence' enabled her to recognise that the violent swings between love and hate, which she had experienced in relation to her father, were a fairly common phenomenon. Though she re-evoked his selfish rages and grotesque behaviour in her late memoir 'A Sketch of the Past', there were moments when all the anger and hatred she had felt towards him in youth vanished and other memories came to the fore. 'How beautiful they were, those old people – I mean father and mother – how simple, how clear, how untroubled. I have been dipping into old letters and father's memoirs. He loved her – oh and was so candid and reasonable and transparent – & had such a fastidious delicate mind, educated and transparent. How serene and gay even their life reads to me. No mud, no whirlpools.'[28]

As has been mentioned, noise created by demolition and building work caused the Woolfs to leave 52 Tavistock Square and move to 37 Mecklenburgh Square shortly before the war began, taking with them the firm of solicitors Dollman & Pritchard. But after Bloomsbury suffered severe bombing in September 1940, a section of Mecklenburgh Square, including their own house, was cordoned off owing to an unexploded bomb. After it had been detonated, the house proved uninhabitable: the windows were blown out, bookcases had come away from the walls, books lay on the floor covered in rubble and plaster, doors hung on single hinges, ceilings had come down and the roof was damaged. The Hogarth Press had to be evacuated to Letchworth in Hertfordshire, and the Woolfs arranged for the removal of what remained of their belongings to Rodmell, where they rented storerooms in two other houses in the village. Rodmell now became for them, in Leonard's words, 'the silent, motionless centre of the hurricane of war'.[29] They continued to make visits to London, and on one of these Virginia confronted again a war-torn city:

We were in London on Monday. I went to London Bridge. I looked at the river; very misty; some tufts of smoke, perhaps from burning houses. There was another fire on Saturday. Then I saw a cliff of wall, eaten out, at one corner; a great corner all smashed; at Bank; the Monument erect; tried to get a Bus; but such a block I dismounted; & the second bus advised me to walk. A complete jam of traffic; for streets were being blown up. So by tube to the Temple; & there wandered in the desolate ruins of my old squares: gashed; dismantled; the old red bricks all white powder, something like a builder's yard; Grey dirt and broken windows; sightseers; all that completeness ravished & demolished. So to Buszards where, for almost the first time, I decided to eat gluttonously. Turkey and pancakes. How rich, how solid. 4/- they cost. And so to the L.L. [London Library] where I collected specimens of English litre [literature].' [30]

Back at Rodmell, Woolf, on at least one occasion, had, at Leonard's instruction, to lie face down in the grass while bomber planes passed overhead, for here too the war came very close. And Monk's House, though it soothed, was damp and untidy, owing to the piles of books that had been salvaged from Mecklenburgh Square. The solitude it offered sometimes led to depressing thoughts. Woolf's diary reads:

'In the cold hour, this, before the lights go up. A few snowdrops in the garden. Yes. I was thinking: we live without a future. That's what's queer, with our noses pressed to a closed door …'[31]

She had not entirely recovered from the bout of depression that had slowed her work on *The Years* in the mid-1930s, and now her health began again to deteriorate. The familiar warning symptoms of forthcoming mental disturbance – headaches, sleeplessness and an inability to concentrate – recurred, and were followed by a trough of despair. She became extremely thin. Now convinced that *Between the Acts* was too 'slight and sketchy', she wrote to John Lehmann to suggest that it ought not to be published. It was put on hold, for Leonard saw that the strain of taking it forward would be more than she could manage – though, as he later told Lehmann, it was, in his opinion, her best book, having more vigour than some of the others.

On 18 November Leonard was alarmed by the fact that she returned from a walk soaking wet. He arranged for her to see Dr Olivia Wilberforce in Brighton a few days later, on 27 March. A physical examination took place, and rest was advised, after which a long conversation between the physician and Leonard took place. The following day, while Leonard was in the garden, Virginia took a walk, leaving two letters on a table in the upstairs sitting-room and a third on her desk in her writing lodge in the garden. Two of these letters were for Leonard; the third, for her sister.[32] Woolf's first authorised biographer Quentin Bell was of the opinion that the letters to Leonard preceded that to Vanessa, and textual analysis would seem to uphold this view. The letter to Vanessa ends:

I can hardly think clearly any more. If I could I would tell you what you and the children have meant to me. I think you know. I have fought against it, but I can't any longer.

Virginia.

It was almost a month before her body was found in the nearby river, with a heavy stone in the pocket of her coat. Leonard, however, had known the manner of her death from the day of her disappearance, for she had left her walking stick on the bank of the river.

In response to a sympathetic letter from Molly MacCarthy, Vanessa wrote: 'One can at least be glad that this did not happen as it so nearly did years ago – when all her gifts would have been wasted.' She went on to acknowledge the person who had done the most to prevent this loss from occurring. 'It is thanks to Leonard that it didn't. He is amazingly sensible and sane.'[33]

Dearest,

You cant think how I loved your letter.
But I feel that I have gone too far this time
to come back again. I am certain now that
I am going mad again. It is just as it was
the first time, I am always hearing voices, &
I know I shant get over it now.

All I want to say is that Leonard has been
so astonishingly good, every day, always;
that I cant imagine that anyone could
have done more for me than he has.
We have been perfectly happy until
the last few weeks, when this horror began.
Will you assure him of this? I feel he has so
much to do that he will go on, better
without me, & you will help him.
I can hardly think clearly any more.
If I could I would tell you what you &
the children have meant to me. I think
you know.
I have fought against it, but I cant
any longer. Virginia

Opposite: Virginia Woolf
with her cocker spaniel,
Pinka, photographed by
Gisèle Freund, 24 June 1939.
The bib Woolf wore for
another photograph, taken
during the sitting (page 12),
can be seen beside her.

Above: Virginia Woolf's
ashes were buried under
one of two great elms in the
garden at Monk's House. One
blew down in 1943, the other
died some years later. The
Woolfs used to refer to them
as 'Leonard' and 'Virginia'.

Opposite: *Still Life with Bust of Virginia Woolf, Charleston* by Duncan Grant, *c.*1960.

Below: Virginia Woolf by Stephen Tomlin, 1931.

NOTES

1   *The Diary of Virginia Woolf, Vol. 4: 1920–24*, ed. Anne Olivier Bell, assisted by Andrew McNeillie (Hogarth Press, London, 1978) p.210.

2   Virginia Woolf, 'A Professor of Life', *Vogue*, early May 1926, p.69. Reprinted in *The Essays of Virginia Woolf, Vol. 4: 1925–1928*, ed. Stuart N. Clarke (Hogarth Press, London, 1982), p.348.

3   Her diary entry for 20 February 1937 refers to her desire to write 'a possible leader on biography', but the most substantial piece she wrote on this subject did not appear until 1939, when she published 'The Art of Biography' in the *Atlantic Monthly*. See *The Essays of Virginia Woolf, Vol. 6: 1933–1941*, ed. Stuart N. Clarke (Chatto & Windus, London, 2012), pp.181–9.

4   Ibid., p.95.

5   The phrase comes from a passage spoken by Shakespeare's Macbeth, after he has murdered Duncan:

Will all great Neptune's ocean wash this blood
Clean from my hand? No, this my hand will rather
The multitudinous seas incarnadine
Making the green one red.

6   *The Essays of Virginia Woolf, Vol. 6*, p.95.

7   See the first chapter titled 'Democratic highbrow: Woolf and the classless intellectual' in Melba Cuddy-Keane, *Virginia Woolf, the Intellectual and the Public Sphere* (Cambridge University Press, Cambridge, 2003), p.13–58. Woolf complained to Ethel Smyth in August 1932 that she was being 'much heckled by journalists for Bloomsbury Highbrowism'. In contrast with these journalistic assumptions, Cuddy-Keane promotes Woolf's interest in a more inclusive and elastic highbrowism, one that engages with a broader community of writers and readers, and gives shape to the diversity needed in a democratic age.

8   *The Essays of Virginia Woolf, Vol. 1: 1904–1912*, ed. Andrew McNeillie (Hogarth Press, London, 1986), p.ix.

9   *The Diary of Virginia Woolf, Vol. 5: 1936–1941*, ed. Anne Olivier Bell, assisted by Andrew McNeillie (Hogarth Press, London, 1984), p.51.

10 *The Diary of Virginia Woolf, Vol. 4*, p.211.

11 Ibid., p.4. 'I could perhaps do B[ernard]'s soliloquy in such a way as to break up, dig deep, make prose move – yes I swear – as prose has never moved before: from the chuckle & the babble to the rhapsody.'

12 Hermione Lee, *Virginia Woolf* (Chatto & Windus, London, 1996), p.659. The recollection of Woolf's impact on others at parties was offered by Anne Olivier Bell, the editor of five volumes of Virginia Woolf's diaries, in conversation with Frances Spalding.

13 *The Diary of Virginia Woolf, Vol. 5*, p.285. See also Lee, *Virginia Woolf*, p.694.

14 *The Diary of Virginia Woolf, Vol. 3: 1925–1930*, ed. Anne Olivier Bell (Hogarth Press, London, 1980), pp.325–6.

15 Virginia Woolf, *A Room of One's Own* (Penguin, London, 2000), p.38.

16 The best source on this complex period within Woolf's career is Virginia Woolf, *The Years*, ed. Anna Snaith (Cambridge University Press, Cambridge, 2013), with its invaluable introduction, notes and textual variants. This scholarly series is edited by Jane Goldman and Susan Sellers, and has already seen the publication of *The Waves* (eds Michael Herbert and Susan Sellers) and *Between the Acts* (ed. Mark Hussey).

17 Almost certainly, these were photographs of the seventy-one children killed when a bomb was dropped on the school in Getafe on 30 October 1936, during Franco's first air-raid on Madrid. The only English newspaper to show these was the *Daily Worker*, which did so on 12 November 1936. Examples of the images Woolf would have received can be found among the International Brigade Archives in the Marx Memorial Library, London.

18 Virginia Woolf, *Three Guineas* (Penguin, London, 1993), p.300. It is found in Chapter 2, note 38, and is one of the reasons why Woolf described her footnotes as 'meaty'.

19 Julian Bell, 'Open Letter to C. Day Lewis', in *Julian Bell: Essays, Poems and Letters*, ed. Quentin Bell (Hogarth Press, London, 1938), p.324.

20 *The Diary of Virginia Woolf, Vol. 5*, p.54.

21 2 April 1941, quoted in Frances Spalding, *Vanessa Bell* (Weidenfeld & Nicolson, London, 1983), p.298.

22 *Leave the Letters Till We're Dead: The Letters of Virginia Woolf, Vol. 6: 1936–1941*, ed. Nigel Nicolson, assisted by Joanne Trautmann

(Hogarth Press, London, 1980), pp.158–9.

23 *The Diary of Virginia Woolf, Vol. 5*, p.292.

24 'No: I intended no introspection. I mark Henry James's sentence: Observe perpetually. Observe the oncome of age. Observe greed. Observe my despondency. By that means it becomes serviceable. Or so I hope …. I will go down with my colours flying.' *The Diary of Virginia Woolf, Vol. 5*, pp.357–8.

25 Ibid., p.17.

26 Gillian Beer, *Arguing with the Past: Essays in Narrative from Woolf to Sydney* (Routledge, London, 1989), p.177.

27 *The Diary of Virginia Woolf, Vol. 5*, p.248.

28 Ibid., p.345.

29 Leonard Woolf, *An Autobiography, Vol. 2: 1911–1969* (Oxford University Press, Oxford, 1980), p.420.

30 *The Diary of Virginia Woolf, Vol. 5*, p.353.

31 Ibid., p.355.

32 At first reading, the content of all three letters suggests that they were written on Friday 28 March, the day of her death. However, none of them is precisely dated. One carries the word 'Tuesday', which has given rise to the suggestion that one of the letters to Leonard was written at an earlier date, and not produced *in extremis* (see Hermione Lee, *Virginia Woolf*, p.756). For further debate about the order and dating of these letters, see Appendix A in *The Letters of Virginia Woolf, Vol. 6*, pp.489–91.

33 Vanessa Bell to Molly MacCarthy, 20 April 1941, King's College Archives, Cambridge. Quoted in Hugh and Mirabel Cecil, *Clever Hearts: Desmond and Molly MacCarthy – A Biography* (Victor Gollancz, London, 1990), p.280.

CHRONOLOGY

1882

Adeline Virginia Stephen born 25 January at 22 Hyde Park Gate, third child of Leslie and Julia Stephen. In addition to her immediate siblings Vanessa and Thoby, there are four other children by her parents' previous marriages, George, Stella and Gerald Duckworth, and Laura Stephen. The family is completed by the arrival of Adrian Stephen in 1883. In November 1882 Leslie Stephen begins editing *The Dictionary of National Biography*, producing the first twenty-six volumes in nine years and writing many of its articles himself.

1882–94

The family spends three to four months each summer surrounded by the sea at Talland House, St Ives, Cornwall.

1891

Laura Stephen is institutionalised.

1892

The Stephen siblings start writing the *Hyde Park Gate News*, an intermittent in-house newspaper that records much about their family life.

Opposite: Virginia Woolf photographed by Barbara Strachey, 1938.

Above: Virginia Stephen, *c.*1893.

Top: (left to right:) Photograph taken after Julia Stephen's death in 1895, showing, back row, Virginia, Vanessa, Thoby and Leslie Stephen wearing black waist-bands or arm-bands. Seated: George Duckworth holding Gurth, Adrian Stephen and Stella Duckworth.

Above: Stella Duckworth, *c*.1896.

1895

Death of Julia Stephen. Virginia Stephen suffers her first breakdown. Her half-sister Stella takes over Julia's maternal role.

1897

In April Stella Duckworth marries Jack Hills and in July dies of peritonitis, aged twenty-eight.

1899

Thoby Stephen enters Trinity College, Cambridge, and makes friends with Lytton Strachey, Saxon Sydney-Turner, Clive Bell and Leonard Woolf, later to become part of the Bloomsbury Group.

1902

Leslie Stephen knighted. Adrian Stephen follows Thoby to Trinity College, Cambridge.

1904

In February Leslie Stephen dies. Following a trip to Venice, Virginia has another, more serious breakdown and makes at least one suicide attempt. She is cared for by Violet Dickinson, at her house at Welwyn, while her Stephen siblings move into 46 Gordon Square, in the Bloomsbury area of London. That autumn Virginia is sufficiently recovered to write a memoir of her father and her first pieces of journalism. She also begins teaching at Morley College.

1904–5

The Stephens hold 'At Homes' on Thursday evenings, to which Thoby invites his Cambridge friends. These form an inner circle that becomes known as 'Bloomsbury'. In 1905 Virginia writes thirty reviews and essays, for the Anglo-Catholic clerical paper, the *Guardian*, for the *Cornhill Magazine* and for the *Times Literary Supplement*. Journalism from now on forms a significant part of her literary output.

1906

The Stephens visit Greece with Violet Dickinson. Vanessa and Thoby fall ill. Once back home Thoby appears to recover, but then suddenly dies. This tragedy draws his friends and relations into closer alliance. Vanessa now accepts a marriage proposal from Clive Bell.

1907

Vanessa and Clive marry. Virginia and Adrian move to 29 Fitzroy

Square where they are near neighbours of Duncan Grant who paints the first oil portrait of Virginia. Begins work on *Melymbrosia* (working title for Woolf's first novel, *The Voyage Out*).

1909

Lytton Strachey proposes marriage and Virginia accepts. The offer is withdrawn within twenty-four hours, without damage to their lasting friendship. Strachey writes to Leonard Woolf in Ceylon, telling him he ought to marry Virginia.

1910

Virginia takes part in the Dreadnought Hoax. She meets Roger Fry at 46 Gordon Square. By the end of this year he has drawn Bloomsbury into a very public debate about art, owing to the brouhaha caused by his exhibition *Manet and the Post-Impressionists*. Over the next few years Virginia witnesses the artistic revolution triggered by the arrival in Britain of modern French art.

1911

Virginia and Adrian move into 38 Brunswick Square, which is shared with Duncan Grant, Maynard Keynes and Leonard Woolf. She visits Rupert Brooke at Grantchester and swims naked with him in the river. A further marriage proposal from Sydney Waterlow is turned down.

1912

Leonard Woolf proposes and is accepted. They marry 10 August. She is thirty; he, thirty-one. They travel in France, Spain and Italy.

1913

Dogged by mental instability, Virginia is temporarily hospitalised. In September, under threat of further hospitalisation, she takes an overdose and has her stomach pumped. Her ill health continues intermittently over a period of three years.

1914

With the onset of war Leonard is spared the decision as to whether or not he should enlist owing to a tremor in his hands and his wife's illness.

1915

Virginia's need for a quiet life causes the Woolfs to exchange Bloomsbury for Richmond and rent Hogarth House. She is too ill to

Top: (left to right:) George and Stella Duckworth with Adrian Stephen and Gurth, the dog, after the death of Julia Stephen, 1895.

Above: (left to right:) Thoby, Adrian, Vanessa and Virginia Stephen, *c*.1896.

Top: Monk's House, Rodmell, *c.*1920–35.

Above: 52 Tavistock Square, *c.*1920–35.

read the reviews of her first novel, *The Voyage Out*, finally published in March. Her condition requires four nurses to be in attendance night and day. By November the nurses have left and Virginia is slowly recovering.

1917

The Woolfs acquire a printing press, which is delivered to their house and the Hogarth Press begins. Virginia typesets many of the early productions. The first, *Two Stories,* includes her experimental 'The Mark on the Wall'. She now begins writing a diary, more or less continuously, for the rest of her life. Her friendship with the writer Katherine Mansfield begins and lasts until Mansfield's death from tuberculosis in 1923.

1918

The Woolfs' friendship with T.S. Eliot begins.

1919

By May, the Hogarth Press's productions include Mansfield's *Prelude*, Woolf's *Kew Gardens* and T.S. Eliot's *Poems*. In September the Woolfs buy Monk's House at Rodmell, in Sussex, which replaces Asheham as their country retreat. In October Virginia publishes her second novel, *Night and Day*.

1920

With the publication of Maxim Gorky's *Reminiscences of Leo Tolstoi*, translated by Samuel Solomonovitch Koteliansky, with assistance from Leonard Woolf, the Hogarth Press embarks on a series of books by Russian authors.

1921

Publication of *Monday or Tuesday*, a collection of Virginia Woolf's short stories.

1922

Publication of Woolf's third novel, *Jacob's Room*. In December she meets Vita Sackville-West.

1923

The Hogarth Press publishes T.S. Eliot's *The Waste Land*, which had first been published the previous year in the October issue of *The Criterion*. Virginia writes her play *Freshwater* (later revised and privately performed in 1935). Visits Spain.

1924

In March, the Woolfs leave Richmond and return to Bloomsbury, taking a lease on 52 Tavistock Square. The Hogarth Press, which has expanded into a commercial business, occupies two floors of this house. The sitting room on its third floor is decorated by Vanessa Bell and Duncan Grant, at Virginia Woolf's request. Her friendship with Vita Sackville-West deepens. It leads to a brief love affair and the brilliantly imaginative *Orlando: A Biography* (1928), in which Woolf's central protagonist is based on Vita.

1925

In May, *Mrs Dalloway*, Woolf's fourth novel, appears, three weeks after her first collection of essays, *The Common Reader*. Her journalism now extends to the high-class fashion magazine *Vogue* and a studio photograph of her appears in the May issue.

1926

A second photograph of Woolf appears in *Vogue*, this time showing her not in a fashionable outfit but in an ill-fitting dress that had belonged to her mother. Simultaneously she is writing *To the Lighthouse*, in which the fictional Mrs Ramsay is given the character of her mother. The revival of interest in the Victorian period is further evidenced by the Hogarth Press publication of *Julia Margaret Cameron: Victorian Photographs of Famous Men and Fair Women*, with essays by Virginia Woolf and Roger Fry.

1927

Fry, an early admirer of Woolf's experimental writing, publishes *Cézanne: A Study of His Development* with the Hogarth Press. Woolf's *To the Lighthouse* is also published this year. The influence of London on her novel-writing is acknowledged in her 'Street Haunting: A London Adventure', published in the *Yale Review*.

1928

Woolf's sixth novel *Orlando: A Biography* is published. Delivers two lectures on 'Women in Fiction' at the Cambridge colleges, Girton and Newnham, which evolve into *A Room of One's Own*.

1929

A Room of One's Own is published. Travels with Leonard to Berlin.

Top: (left to right:) Benedict Nicolson, Virginia Woolf, Vita Sackville-West and Nigel Nicolson at Sissinghurst Castle, *c.*1920–35.

Above: Virginia Woolf and Vita Sackville West, *c.*1920–35.

1930

Friendship with Ethel Smyth begins.

1931

The Waves is published. Sits to the sculptor Stephen Tomlin for a portrait bust. Tours France, again with Leonard.

1932

Lytton Strachey dies, and soon after Dora Carrington commits suicide. *The Common Reader*, a second collection of Woolf's essays, is published.

1933

Flush, Woolf's biography of Elizabeth Barrett Browning's dog, appears.

1934

Sits for photo-portraits by Man Ray. Death of Roger Fry.

1935

During the rewriting of her historical novel *The Years*, Woolf suffers another breakdown. In May, Leonard takes her to Cornwall for a break.

1936

Finishes *The Years*. Collapses in April. Ill health returns June to October. Onset of Spanish Civil War stimulates in her nephew Julian Bell a desire to fight for democracy against fascism. He is persuaded instead to work for Spanish Medical Aid as an ambulance driver. In the wake of the bombing of Getafe, Woolf receives photographs of dead children in the post. How to prevent war becomes the driving question behind her writing of *Three Guineas*.

Top: Lytton Strachey and Virginia Woolf at Garsington. Photographed by Lady Ottoline Morrell, June 1923.

Above: Roger Fry in Greece, 1932.

1937

The Years is published in March. In July Julian Bell, aged twenty-nine, is killed by shrapnel in Spain. Woolf attends Vanessa Bell daily as she slowly recovers from the complete breakdown brought on by news of her son's death. Begins work on her biography of Roger Fry, written at the request of his sister Margery Fry.

1938

Three Guineas is published. She sells her half-ownership of the Hogarth Press to John Lehmann.

1939

Gisèle Freund photographs the Woolfs in colour at 52 Tavistock Square on 24 June, shortly before they move to 37 Mecklenburgh Square. Woolf now divides her writing time between the biography of Roger Fry and the novel *Between the Acts*.

1940

In July *Roger Fry* is published. In the autumn Blitz 52 Tavistock Square is completely destroyed and 37 Mecklenburgh Square severely damaged. Woolf salvages her diaries from the latter. From then on she and Leonard make Monk's House their permanent home.

1941

Revises *Between the Acts* but judges it to be unpublishable. Drowns herself in the River Ouse on 28 March. *Between the Acts* is published posthumously.

Above: Leonard Woolf, *c.*1920–35.

Left: (left to right:) Angelica Bell, Vanessa Bell, Clive Bell, Virginia Woolf and John Maynard Keynes outside the writing hut at Monk's House, *c.*1920–35.

Below, left: Virginia Woolf outside her writing hut at Monk's House, Rodmell, with Dr Noel Richard and her daughter, Virginia, *c.*1930s.

Below, right: Virginia Woolf photographed by Barbara Strachey, 1938.

FURTHER READING

Books on or by Virginia Woolf are widely available. In recent years Vintage, Penguin and Oxford University Press have all promoted her novels in paperback, many of which are introduced and sometimes edited by leading writers and academics. Woolf's diaries are an invaluable resource on her own life and work, and the insights they offer are further supplemented by the many letters she wrote, and by her essays, all of which have been collected and published. What follows is a list of her own publications, then a further selection of books from the vast literature available, which offer particular insights on aspects of her life and work.

BY VIRGINIA WOOLF

The Voyage Out (1915), ed. Lorna Sage (Oxford University Press, Oxford, 2001)

Night and Day (1919), ed. Suzanne Raitt (Oxford University Press, Oxford, 1992)

Jacob's Room (1922), ed. Kate Flint (Oxford University Press, Oxford, 2005)

The Common Reader (1925; Vintage, London, 2003)

Mrs Dalloway (1925), ed. David Bradshaw (Oxford University Press, Oxford, 2008)

To the Lighthouse (1927), ed. David Bradshaw (Oxford University Press, Oxford, 2006)

Orlando: A Biography (1928), ed. Rachel Bowlby (Oxford University Press, Oxford, 1992)

A Room of One's Own (1928), ed. Morag Shiach (Oxford University Press, Oxford, 1998)

The Waves (1931), ed. Gillian Beer (Oxford University Press, Oxford, 1992)

The Common Reader II (1932; Vintage, London, 2003)

Flush (1933), ed. Kate Flint (Oxford University Press, Oxford, 1998)

The Years (1937), ed. Hermione Lee (Oxford University Press, Oxford, 1992)

Roger Fry: A Biography (1940; Vintage, London, 2003)

Between the Acts (1941), ed. Frank Kermode (Oxford University Press, Oxford, 1992)

The Letters of Virginia Woolf, 6 vols, ed. Nigel Nicolson, assisted by Joanne Trautmann Banks (Hogarth Press, London, 1975–80)

Moments of Being, ed. Jeanne Schulkind (1976), revised by Hermione Lee (Pimlico, London, 2002)

The Diary of Virginia Woolf, 5 vols, ed. Anne Olivier Bell, assisted by Andrew McNeillie (1977–84), (Penguin, Harmondsworth, 1979–85)

The Essays of Virginia Woolf, Vols 1–3 ed. Andrew McNeillie, Vols 4–6 ed. Stuart N. Clarke (Hogarth Press, London, 1986–2011)

A Passionate Apprentice: The Early Journals of Virginia Woolf, ed. Mitchell A. Leaska (Hogarth Press, London, 1990)

BIOGRAPHIES OF VIRGINIA WOOLF

The first official biographer of Virginia Woolf was her nephew Quentin Bell, who laid down, in two volumes, the central narrative of her life and work. Twenty-four years later, in 1996, Hermione Lee, incorporating not only new research but also awareness of the multiplicity of debates that had developed around Woolf, published what has become the standard 900-page biography of her. More than a dozen other biographies of Woolf exist, and to be recommended are those by Lyndall Gordon (1984) and Julia Briggs (2005), as well as Alexandra Harris's short life (2011). First-hand information on Virginia Woolf can also be found in Leonard Woolf's autobiography (published in five volumes by Hogarth Press, London, 1960–9), which remains a key source on many aspects of their life together and on the formation of the Bloomsbury Group.

GENERAL AND SPECIALIST READING ON VIRGINIA WOOLF

Gillian Beer, *Arguing with the Past: Essays in Narrative from Woolf to Sidney* (Routledge, London, 1989)
Virginia Woolf: The Common Ground (Edinburgh University Press, Edinburgh, 1996)

Vanessa Bell, *Notes on Virginia's Childhood: A Memoir*, ed. Richard J. Schaubeck Jr (F. Hallman, New York, 1974)

Pamela L. Caughie, ed., *Virginia Woolf in the Age of Mechanical Reproduction* (Garland, New York, 2000)

Melba Cuddy-Keane, *Virginia Woolf, the Intellectual and the Public Sphere* (Cambridge University Press, Cambridge, 2003)

Vanessa Curtis, *Virginia Woolf's Women* (Sutton Publishing, Stroud, 2002)

Diane F. Gillespie, *The Sisters' Arts: The Writing and Painting of Virginia Woolf and Vanessa Bell* (Syracuse University Press, New York, 1988)

Jane Goldman, *The Cambridge Introduction to Virginia Woolf* (Cambridge University Press, Cambridge, 2006)

Nuala Hancock, *Charleston and Monk's House: The Intimate House Museums of Vanessa Bell and Virginia Woolf* (Edinburgh University Press, Edinburgh, 2012)

Maggie Humm, ed., *The Edinburgh Companion to Virginia Woolf and the Arts* (Edinburgh University Press, Edinburgh, 2010)
Modernist Women and Visual Cultures: Virginia Woolf, Vanessa Bell, Photography and Cinema (Edinburgh University Press, Edinburgh, 1992)

Hermione Lee, *The Novels of Virginia Woolf* (Methuen, London, 1977)

Alison Light, *Mrs Woolf and the Servants: The Hidden Heart of Domestic Service* (Fig Tree, London, 2007)

Laura Marcus, *Writers and Their Work: Virginia Woolf* (Northcote, Tonbridge, 1997, revised 2004)

Jean Moorcroft Wilson, *Virginia Woolf: Life and London: A Biography of Place* (Cecil Woolf, London, 1987)

Joan Russell Noble, ed., *Recollections of Virginia Woolf* (Penguin, Harmondsworth, 1972; with an introduction by Michael Holroyd, 1975)

Bryony Randall and Jane Goldman, eds, *Virginia Woolf in Context* (Cambridge University Press, Cambridge, 2012)

Susan Sellers, ed., *The Cambridge Companion to Virginia Woolf* (Cambridge University Press, Cambridge, 2000, revised 2010)

Brenda R. Silver, *Virginia Woolf Icon* (Chicago University Press, Chicago, 1999)
Virginia Woolf's Reading Notebooks (Princeton University Press, New Jersey, 1983)

Angela Smith, *Katherine Mansfield and Virginia Woolf: A Public of Two* (Clarendon Press, Oxford, 1999)

Anna Snaith and Michael H. Whitworth, eds, *Locating Woolf: The Politics of Space and Place* (Palgrave/Macmillan, Basingstoke, 2007)

Helen Southworth, ed., *Leonard and Virginia Woolf, the Hogarth Press and the Networks of Modernism* (Edinburgh University Press, Edinburgh, 2010)

Caroline Zoob, *Virginia Woolf's Garden: The Story of the Garden at Monk's House* (Jacqui Small, London, 2013)

ACKNOWLEDGEMENTS

Virginia Woolf is one of the greatest writers of all time and a major cultural phenomenon. The opportunity to work with the National Portrait Gallery on this exhibition has been a daunting but hugely enjoyable task, and in this I have been greatly helped by a number of people. I wish to express my thanks to its Director, Sandy Nairne, and to the staff who have formed an enormously supportive team around this project, namely: Sarah Tinsley, Paul Moorhouse, Rosie Wilson, Ulrike Wachsmann, Terence Pepper, and especially to Flora Fricker, the Exhibitions Manager, who has been central in guiding and steering all the decisions that had to be made. I am grateful, too, for the alacrity with which Claudia Tobin has acted as research assistant, and for the perceptive and imaginative design that Calum Storrie has brought to the exhibition. I would also like to thank Andrew Roff, Christopher Tinker and Nicola Saunders, in Publications, for their expert handling of the details in connection with the making of the book, Patricia Burgess for her sure hand as copy-editor, and Ruth Müller-Wirth, Mark Fairman, Helen Trompeteler and Ruth Slaney for their work on the reproductions. Conversations with many others about Woolf and her writings have been a source of great stimulus, and in particular I would like to mention Dame Gillian Beer, Lucy Gent, Alexandra Harris, Dame Hermione Lee, Susan Sellers and Richard Shone. The generosity of the various lenders to this exhibition has been a source of enormous encouragement. I am also greatly indebted to many curators, archivists and librarians who have assisted my research, and in particular to Karen Kukil, the Associate Curator of Special Collections at Smith College, Massachusetts, Dale Stinchcombe, Curatorial Assistant of the Harvard Theatre Collection in the Houghton Library, Harvard University, and to Isaac Gewirtz, Curator of the Berg Collection in New York Public Library.

PICTURE CREDITS

Page 2 Virginia Woolf
Unknown photographer, 1927
Courtesy of the Mortimer Rare Book Room, Neilson Library, Smith College, Northampton, Massachusetts

Page 8 *Three Guineas* by Virginia Woolf, Hogarth Press, 1938
Cover design by Vanessa Bell
Book, 210 x 148
© Estate of Vanessa Bell, courtesy of Henrietta Garnett
Image: Victoria University Library

Page 11 Virginia Stephen
George Charles Beresford, July 1902
Platinum prints, each 152 x 108
© National Portrait Gallery, London

(clockwise from top left: NPG P221, P222, P223, P220)

Page 12 Virginia Woolf
Gisèle Freund, 24 June 1939
Colour dye transfer print, 300 x 200
Private Collection, Penelope Cordish
Image by Mitro Hood © Gisèle Freund/IMEC/Fonds MCC

Page 14 'Modern English Decoration' article in *Vogue*, early November 1924
Magazine, 297 x 210 closed
Vogue © The Condé Nast Publications Ltd

Page 16 Virginia and Leonard Woolf
Gisèle Freund with their cocker spaniel, Pinka, 24 June 1939
Colour dye transfer print, 301 x 201
National Portrait Gallery, Purchased, 1990 (NPG P439)
© Estate Gisèle Freund/IMEC Images

Page 17 52 Tavistock Square after a hit from a bomb in October 1940
Unknown photographer, April 1941
Vogue © The Condé Nast Publications Ltd

Page 18 A page from Virginia Woolf's diary, 20 October 1940
The Henry W. and Albert A. Berg Collection of English and American Literature, The New York Public Library, Astor, Lenox and Tilden Foundations

Page 19 Above, left: Original watercolour sketch for dust jacket

of *A Writer's Diary*
Vanessa Bell, n.d.
Watercolour on paper, 216 x 127
The Henry W. and Albert A. Berg Collection of English and American Literature, The New York Public Library, Astor, Lenox and Tilden Foundations.
© Estate of Vanessa Bell, courtesy of Henrietta Garnett

Above, right: *A Writer's Diary* by Virginia Woolf, Hogarth Press, 1953.
Cover design by Vanessa Bell
Book, 210 x 148
© Estate of Vanessa Bell, courtesy of Henrietta Garnett

Page 20 *The Diary of Virginia Woolf Volume III, 1925–1930*, Hogarth Press, 1980. Cover design by Duncan Grant
© Estate of Duncan Grant. All rights reserved, DACS 2014

Page 22 Vanessa Stephen painting, with Virginia seated beside her, and (left to right) Thoby and Adrian behind
Stella Duckworth, c.1896
The Henry W. and Albert A. Berg Collection of English and American Literature, The New York Public Library, Astor, Lenox and Tilden Foundations

Page 24 *The Memoir Club*
Vanessa Bell, c.1943
Oil on canvas, 608 x 816
© Estate of Vanessa Bell, courtesy of Henrietta Garnett. National Portrait Gallery, London (NPG 6718)

Library, Astor, Lenox and Tilden
Foundations

*Page 55 Violet Dickinson's home
Burnham Wood at Welwyn in
Hertfordshire
Unknown photographer, c.1904
The Henry W. and Albert A. Berg
Collection of English and American
Literature, The New York Public
Library, Astor, Lenox and Tilden
Foundations

*Page 57 Caroline Emilia Stephen
Unknown photographer, c.1880s
Courtesy of the Mortimer Rare
Book Room, Neilson Library,
Smith College, Northampton,
Massachusetts

*Page 58 Sir Leslie Stephen
Photogravure reproduction by Emery
Walker after photograph by George
Charles Beresford, December 1902
Courtesy of the Mortimer Rare
Book Room, Neilson Library,
Smith College, Northampton,
Massachusetts

*Page 60 Henry James
William Rothenstein, 1898
Lithograph, 250 x 202, (P.9682-R)
© The Fitzwilliam Museum,
Cambridge

*Page 61 Thoby Stephen
George Charles Beresford, August
1906
Vintage photograph, 152 x 106
Courtesy of the Mortimer Rare
Book Room, Neilson Library,
Smith College, Northampton,
Massachusetts

*Page 63 Adrian Stephen
Duncan Grant, c.1911–12
Oil on canvas, 335 x 250
The Charleston Trust
Image: © Estate of Duncan Grant.
All rights reserved, DACS 2014

*Page 64 Virginia Stephen
Duncan Grant, c.1911
Oil on panel (masonite), 564 x 410
Lent by The Metropolitan Museum
of Art, Purchase, Lila Acheson
Wallace Gift, 1990 (1990.236)
© 2013. Image copyright The
Metropolitan Museum of
Art/Art Resource/Scala, Florence
Image: © Estate of Duncan Grant.
All rights reserved, DACS 2014

*Page 65 Virginia Stephen at
Fitzroy Square

Duncan Grant, c.1909
Pen and ink, 375 x 320
Mrs Quentin Bell
Image: © Estate of Duncan Grant.
All rights reserved, DACS 2014

*Page 66 Lytton Strachey
Simon Bussy, 1904
Pastel, 533 x 432
© reserved; collection National
Portrait Gallery, London (NPG 4595)

*Page 67 Lytton Strachey and
Virginia Woolf at Garsington
Lady Ottoline Morrell, June 1923
Vintage snapshot print, 62 x 105
National Portrait Gallery, London
(NPG Ax141463)

*Page 68 Letter from Lytton Strachey
to Virginia Stephen, 17 February 1909
Original letter, 297 x 210
Courtesy of the Mortimer Rare
Book Room, Neilson Library,
Smith College, Northampton,
Massachusetts

*Page 69 Saxon Sydney-Turner
at the piano
Vanessa Bell, c.1908
Oil on canvas, 185 x 240
The Charleston Trust
Image: © The Estate of Vanessa Bell
courtesy of Henrietta Garnett

Page 70 Above, left: Virginia Stephen
Francis Dodd, 1908
Chalk drawing, 203 x 165
© National Portrait Gallery, London
(NPG 3802)

Above, right: Virginia Stephen
Francis Dodd, 1909
Drypoint etching, 278 x 153
© estate of Francis Dodd
Image © The Trustees of the British
Museum

*Page 72 Roger Fry
Vanessa Bell, 1912
Oil on panel, 293 x 236
© Estate of Vanessa Bell, courtesy of
Henrietta Garnett; National Portrait
Gallery, London (NPG 6684)

*Page 73 James Strachey
Duncan Grant, 1910
Oil on canvas, 635 x 762
Tate: Purchased 1947
Image: © Tate, London 2014
© Estate of Duncan Grant. All rights
reserved, DACS 2014

*Page 74 Leonard Woolf
Henry Lamb, 1912

Oil on canvas, 512 x 410
Private Collection

*Page 76 Leonard Woolf and Virginia
Stephen, visiting Dalingridge, in
Sussex, the home of George and
Margaret Duckworth
Unknown photographer, 1912
Exhibition print, Courtesy of
the Mortimer Rare Book Room,
Neilson Library, Smith College,
Northampton, Massachusetts

*Page 77 Letter from Leonard
and Virginia to Lytton Strachey
announcing their engagement,
6 June 1912
Original letter, 297 x 210
Courtesy of the Mortimer Rare
Book Room, Neilson Library, Smith
College, Northampton, Massachusetts

*Page 78 Virginia Woolf
Roger Fry, 1911–12
Oil on board, 420 x 320
Private Collection

*Page 79 Virginia Woolf
Vanessa Bell, c.1912
Oil on panel, 550 x 450 x 30
Monk's House, Rodmell, The
Virginia & Leonard Woolf Collection
(National Trust)
© Estate of Vanessa Bell, courtesy of
Henrietta Garnett
Image © National Trust/
Charles Thomas

*Page 80 Virginia Woolf in an
armchair
Vanessa Bell, c.1912
Oil on board, 400 x 340
© National Portrait Gallery, London
(NPG 5933)

Page 81 Virginia Woolf
Vanessa Bell, c.1912
Oil on paperboard, 368 x 305
Smith College Museum of Art,
Northampton, Massachusetts. Gift
of Ann Safford Mandel, class of 1953
© Estate of Vanessa Bell, courtesy of
Henrietta Garnett

Page 82 Virginia Woolf in a
deckchair
Vanessa Bell, c.1912
Oil on board, 348 x 240
Private Collection
© Estate of Vanessa Bell, courtesy
of Henrietta Garnett

*Pages 84–5 Conversation at
Asheham House
Vanessa Bell, 1912

Oil on board, 620 x 765
© University of Hull Art Collection, Humberside, UK/The Bridgeman Art Library. © Estate of Vanessa Bell, courtesy of Henrietta Garnett

Page 86 Asheham House, Sussex
Unknown photographer, c.1911
MS Thr 564, Harvard Theatre Collection, Houghton Library, Harvard University

*Page 88 *Spring Morning* (1915) by Frances Cornford with illustrations by Gwen Raverat, and annotations by Virginia Woolf
Book, 210 x 155
The Society of Authors as the Literary Representative of the Estate of Virginia Woolf

*Page 92 *The Conversation*
Vanessa Bell, 1913–16
Oil on canvas, 866 x 810
The Samuel Courtauld Trust, The Courtauld Gallery, London
© The Samuel Courtauld Trust/1961 Estate of Vanessa Bell, courtesy of Henrietta Garnett

*Page 94 Above, left: 'The Mark on the Wall' by Virginia Woolf, in *Two Stories*, Hogarth Press, 1917
Book, 148 x 105
Courtesy of the Mortimer Rare Book Room, Neilson Library, Smith College, Northampton, Massachusetts

*Above, right: *Prelude* by Katherine Mansfield, Hogarth Press, July 1917. Cover design by John Duncan Fergusson
Book, 148 x 105
Victoria University Library
© The Fergusson Gallery, Perth and Kinross Council, Scotland

*Page 95 Hope Mirrlees
Simon Bussy, c.1919
Pastel on paper, 304 x 457
Private Collection

*Page 96 *The Waste Land* by T.S. Eliot, Hogarth Press, 1923
Book, 230 x 145
Victoria University Library

*Page 97 Virginia Woolf with Vivienne and T.S. Eliot at Monk's House, Rodmell, Sussex
Leonard Woolf, 1932
Harvard Theatre Collection, Houghton Library, Harvard University

*Pages 98–9 *Paris* by Hope Mirrlees, Hogarth Press, 1920
Book, 150 x 115
Private Collection
© Literary Executor of Hope Mirrlees

*Page 101 T.S. Eliot and Virginia Woolf in the Green Room, Garsington
Lady Ottoline Morrell, June 1924
Vintage snapshot print, 93 x 75
© National Portrait Gallery, London (NPG Ax141646)

*Page 102 Hogarth Press bill addressed to Lytton Strachey, 11 November 1924, 297 x 210
Courtesy of the Mortimer Rare Book Room, Neilson Library, Smith College, Northampton, Massachusetts

*Pages 104–5 *Kew Gardens* by Virginia Woolf, Hogarth Press, 1919
Woodcut illustrations by Vanessa Bell
Book, 148 x 105
Courtesy of the Mortimer Rare Book Room, Neilson Library, Smith College, Northampton, Massachusetts

Page 106 *Still Life with Apples*
Paul Cézanne, c.1878
Oil on canvas, 190 x 270
© The Provost and Fellows of King's College, Cambridge

*Page 107 *The Matisse Room, Second Post-Impressionist Exhibition*
Roger Fry, 1912
Oil on board, 505 x 605
Paris, Musée d'Orsay, donated by Mme Pamela Diamand, daughter of the artist, 1959

*Page 109 Katherine Mansfield
Adelphi Studios Ltd., 60 Strand, London, 1913
Modern print from half-plate (glass copy) negative, 162 x 120
© National Portrait Gallery, London (NPG x88511)

*Page 111 Samuel Solomonovitch Koteliansky
Mark Gertler, 1930
Oil on canvas, 700 x 900
Private Collection

*Page 112 *Jacob's Room* by Virginia Woolf, Hogarth Press, 1922. Cover design by Vanessa Bell
Book, 210 x 148
© Estate of Vanessa Bell, courtesy of

Henrietta Garnett
Image: Victoria University Library

*Page 114 Virginia Woolf at Garsington
Lady Ottoline Morrell, June 1926
Vintage snapshot print, 118 x 64
© National Portrait Gallery, London (NPG Ax142591)

*Page 116 Above: Card announcing Vanessa Bell and Duncan Grant's interest in receiving commissions for decorative schemes, Christmas 1922
Card, 45 x 55
Courtesy of the Mortimer Rare Book Room, Neilson Library, Smith College, Northampton, Massachusetts

Right: The fireplace in the sitting-room at Tavistock Square, showing one of the wall decorations designed by Bell and Grant and the firescreen designed by Grant
Unknown photographer, 1924
© Tate, London 2014
© Estate of Duncan Grant. All rights reserved, DACS 2014

*Page 117 Above, left: *Monday or Tuesday* by Virginia Woolf, Hogarth Press, 1921. Cover design by Vanessa Bell
Book, 210 x 148
© Estate of Vanessa Bell, courtesy of Henrietta Garnett
Image: Victoria University Library

*Above, right: 'The String Quartet' woodcut by Vanessa Bell, from *Monday or Tuesday*, 1921
Page from book, 210 x 148
© Estate of Vanessa Bell, courtesy of Henrietta Garnett
Image: Victoria University Library

*Page 118 *Mrs Dalloway* by Virginia Woolf, Hogarth Press, 1925. Cover design by Vanessa Bell
Book, 210 x 148
© Estate of Vanessa Bell, courtesy of Henrietta Garnett
Image: Victoria University Library

*Page 119 Sir Desmond MacCarthy
Duncan Grant, 1944
Oil on canvas, 914 x 845
National Portrait Gallery, London (NPG 4842)
Image: © Estate of Duncan Grant. All rights reserved, DACS 2014

*Page 120 *Rush Hour*
Sybil Andrews, 1930

Linocut, 209 x 251
Collection Gilda & John P. McGarry Jr.

*Page 121 *Piccadilly Circus Underground*
Douglas MacPherson, 1928
Poster, 700 x 615
© TfL from the London Transport Museum collection

*Page 122 *The Waves* by Virginia Woolf, Hogarth Press, 1932.
Cover design by Vanessa Bell
Book, 210 x 148
© Estate of Vanessa Bell, courtesy Henrietta Garnett
Image: Victoria University Library

*Page 124 Vita Sackville-West at Sissinghurst Castle
Gisèle Freund, 1939
Colour dye transfer print, 304 x 208
National Portrait Gallery, London (NPG P437)
© Estate Gisèle Freund/IMEC Images

*Page 126 Virginia Woolf
Maurice Beck and Helen Macgregor for *Vogue* magazine, late May 1925
Vogue © The Condé Nast Publications Ltd

*Page 127 Virginia Woolf wearing her mother's dress
Maurice Beck and Helen Macgregor for *Vogue* magazine, early May 1926
Vogue © The Condé Nast Publications Ltd

*Page 129 Madge Garland
Edward Wolfe, 1926
Oil on canvas, 813 x 559
The Geffrye, Museum of the Home
© The Estate of Edward Wolfe/ Geffrye Museum, London

*Pages 130–1 Maurice Bowra and Virginia Woolf at Garsington
Lady Ottoline Morrell, June 1926
Vintage snapshot prints, 118 x 64
© National Portrait Gallery, London (NPG Ax142595 and Ax142593)

*Pages 132–3 Philip Nichols, Virginia Woolf and Philip Morrell at Garsington
Lady Ottoline Morrell, June 1926
Vintage snapshot print, 78 x 117
© National Portrait Gallery, London (NPG Ax142586)

*Page 133 Virginia Woolf at Garsington
Lady Ottoline Morrell, June 1926
Vintage snapshot print, 116 x 68

© National Portrait Gallery, London (NPG Ax142592)

*Page 134 Virginia Woolf at Garsington
Lady Ottoline Morrell, June 1926
Vintage snapshot print, 118 x 67
© National Portrait Gallery, London (NPG Ax142597)

*Pages 134–5 Virginia Woolf at Garsington
Lady Ottoline Morrell, June 1926
Vintage snapshot print, 78 x 66
© National Portrait Gallery, London (NPG Ax142604)

*Page 135 Virginia Woolf at Garsington
Lady Ottoline Morrell, June 1926
Vintage snapshot print, 107 x 69
© National Portrait Gallery, London (NPG Ax142598)

*Page 137 *To the Lighthouse* by Virginia Woolf, Hogarth Press, 1927.
Cover design by Vanessa Bell
Book, 210 x 148
© Estate of Vanessa Bell, courtesy of Henrietta Garnett
Image: Victoria University Library

*Page 138 Roger Fry
Lenare, 1920s
Chlorobromide print, 355 x 263
The Bloomsbury Workshop

*Page 139 *Cézanne: A Study of His Development* by Roger Fry, Hogarth Press, 1927
Book, 148 x 105
Image: Victoria University Library

*Pages 140–1 Pages from the original manuscript of *A Room of One's Own* with the working title *Women in Fiction*, 1928–9
Manuscript, 270 x 210, (MS 1-1942)
© The Fitzwilliam Museum, Cambridge

*Page 142 *A Room of One's Own* by Virginia Woolf, Hogarth Press, 1929.
Cover design by Vanessa Bell
Book, 210 x 148
© Estate of Vanessa Bell, courtesy of Henrietta Garnett
Image: Victoria University Library

*Page 144 Virginia Woolf
Man Ray at his temporary London studio at the offices of the Lund Humphries publishing house, 27 November 1934
Photograph, 230 x 175
Museum Ludwig Cologne/

Collection Gruber
© Rheinisches Bildarchiv Cologne, rba_158948
© Man Ray Trust/ADAGP, Paris and DACS, London 2014

*Page 149 Dame Ethel Smyth
Bassano Ltd., 11 March 1927
Exhibition print from whole plate negative, 254 x 304
© National Portrait Gallery, London (NPG x18838)

*Page 151 Above, left: *The Years* by Virginia Woolf, Hogarth Press, 1937.
Cover design by Vanessa Bell
Book, 210 x 148
© Estate of Vanessa Bell, courtesy of Henrietta Garnett
Image: Victoria University Library

*Above, right: 'This is what Fascism Means!', 30 October 1936
International Brigade pamphlet, 270 x 210
Marx Memorial Library

*Page 152 Julian Bell
Unknown photographer, *c.*1935
Harvard Theatre Collection, Houghton Library, Harvard University

*Page 153 Vanessa Bell
Duncan Grant, *c.*1935
Oil on collage on canvas, 690 x 735
Mrs Quentin Bell
Image: © Estate of Duncan Grant. All rights reserved, DACS 2014

*Page 154 *Weeping Woman*
Pablo Picasso, 1937
Graphite and crayon on paper, 292 x 232
Tate: Accepted by HM Government in lieu of tax and allocated to the Tate Gallery 1995
Image: © Succession Picasso/DACS, London 2014

*Page 156 Poster for Picasso's *Guernica* exhibition at New Burlington Galleries, 1938
Poster, 316 x 202
Roland Penrose Archive, Scottish National Gallery of Modern Art, Edinburgh

*Page 157 *Between the Acts* by Virginia Woolf, Hogarth Press, 1941.
Cover design by Vanessa Bell
Book, 210 x 148
© Estate of Vanessa Bell, courtesy Henrietta Garnett
Image: Victoria University Library

*Page 159 Sigmund Freud at his home 20 Maresfield Gardens, Hampstead Unknown photographer, 1939

*Page 160 Letter from Leonard to Freud's daughter Anna, 26 September 1939
Freud Museum London

*Page 163 Virginia Woolf's letter to Vanessa Bell, 1941
Letter, 297 x 210
The British Library
© The British Library Board

*Page 164 Virginia Woolf with her cocker spaniel, Pinka
Gisèle Freund, 24 June 1939
© Gisèle Freund/IMEC/Fonds MCC

Page 165 Virginia Woolf's ashes were buried under one of two great elms in the garden at Monk's House.
Photographer unknown, *c*.1920–35
MS Thr 584, Harvard Theatre Collection, Houghton Library, Harvard University

*Page 166 *Still Life with Bust of Virginia Woolf, Charleston*
Duncan Grant, *c*.1960
Oil on canvas, 760 x 503
Collection Bryan Ferry
Image: © Estate of Duncan Grant.
All rights reserved,
DACS 2014

*Page 167 Virginia Woolf
Stephen Tomlin, 1931
Painted plaster, 410 x 390 x 220
© Penelope Fewster. Courtesy of Charleston

Page 170 Virginia Woolf
Barbara Strachey, 1938
Bromide print, 81 x 80
© National Portrait Gallery, London (NPG Ax125376)

Page 171 Virginia Stephen
Unknown photographer, *c*.1893
The Henry W. and Albert A. Berg Collection of English and American Literature, The New York Public Library, Astor, Lenox and Tilden Foundations

Page 172 Top: Back row: Virginia, Vanessa, Thoby and Leslie Stephen wearing black waist-bands or arm-bands. Seated: George Duckworth holding Gurth, Adrian Stephen and Stella Duckworth
Unknown photographer, 1895
The Henry W. and Albert A. Berg Collection of English and American Literature, The New York Public Library, Astor, Lenox and Tilden Foundations

Above: Stella Duckworth
Unknown photographer, *c*.1896
The Henry W. and Albert A. Berg Collection of English and American Literature, The New York Public Library, Astor, Lenox and Tilden Foundations

Page 173 Top: George and Stella Duckworth with Adrian Stephen and Gurth, the dog, after the death of Julia Stephen, 1895
Unknown photographer, 1895
The Henry W. and Albert A. Berg Collection of English and American Literature, The New York Public Library, Astor, Lenox and Tilden Foundations

Above: Thoby, Adrian, Vanessa and Virginia Stephen
Unknown photographer, *c*.1896
The Henry W. and Albert A. Berg Collection of English and American Literature, The New York Public Library, Astor, Lenox and Tilden Foundations

Page 174 Top: Monk's House, Rodmell
Unknown photographer, *c*.1920–35
MS Thr 564, Harvard Theatre Collection, Houghton Library, Harvard University

Below: 52 Tavistock Square
Unknown photographer, *c*.1920–35
MS Thr 564, Harvard Theatre Collection, Houghton Library, Harvard University

Page 175 Top: Benedict Nicolson, Virginia Woolf, Vita Sackville-West

and Nigel Nicolson at Sissinghurst Castle
Unknown photographer, *c*.1920–35

Above: Virginia Woolf and Vita Sackville West
Unknown photographer, *c*.1920–35
MS Thr 564, Harvard Theatre Collection, Houghton Library, Harvard University

Page 176 Top: Lytton Strachey and Virginia Woolf at Garsington
Lady Ottoline Morrell, June 1923
Vintage snapshot print, 135 x 83
National Portrait Gallery, London (NPG Ax141460)

Above: Roger Fry in Greece
Unknown photographer, 1932
MS Thr 564, Harvard Theatre Collection, Houghton Library, Harvard University

Page 177 Above: Leonard Woolf
Unknown photographer, *c*.1920–35
MS Thr 564, Harvard Theatre Collection, Houghton Library, Harvard University

Left: Angelica Bell, Vanessa Bell, Clive Bell, Virginia Woolf and John Maynard Keynes outside the writing hut at Monk's House, Rodmell
Unknown photographer, *c*.1920–35
MS Thr 564, Harvard Theatre Collection, Houghton Library, Harvard University

Below, left Virginia Woolf outside her writing hut at Monk's House, Rodmell, with Dr Noel Richard and her daughter, Virginia
Photographer unknown, *c*.1930s
MS Thr 564, Harvard Theatre Collection, Houghton Library, Harvard University

Below, right: Virginia Woolf
Barbara Strachey, 1938
Bromide print, 105 x 101
© National Portrait Gallery, London (NPG Ax88536)

INDEX

Published in Great Britain by
National Portrait Gallery Publications
St Martin's Place, London WC2H 0HE

Published to accompany the exhibition *Virginia Woolf: Art, Life and Vision*
at the National Portrait Gallery, London, from 10 July to 26 October 2014.

This exhibition has been made possible by the provision of insurance
through the Government Indemnity Scheme. The National Portrait Gallery,
London, would like to thank HM Government for providing Government
Indemnity and the Department for Culture, Media and Sport and Arts
Council England for arranging the indemnity.

With thanks to the *Virginia Woolf: Art, Life and Vision* Exhibition Supporter
Group and the T.S. Eliot Estate.

For a complete catalogue of current publications, please write to the National
Portrait Gallery at the address above, or visit our website at
www.npg.org/publications

ISBN 978 1 85514 481 1

A catalogue record for this book is available from the British Library.

10 9 8 7 6 5 4 3 2

Printed in Italy

Managing Editor: Christopher Tinker
Editor: Andrew Roff
Copy-editor: Patricia Burgess
Production Manager: Ruth Müller-Wirth
Design: Lisa Pettibone

Page 2: Virginia Woolf by an unknown photographer, 1927. Pages 4–5:
T.S. Eliot and Virginia Woolf at Garsington photographed by Lady Ottoline
Morrell, June 1924 (detail of image on page 101). Page 6: Virginia Woolf by
Roger Fry, 1911–12 (detail of image on page 78).